Louisiana Projectile Points: Identification & Geographic Range

Christopher A. Cameron

© 2020 Field Technologies, Inc. All rights reserved.

Published by Field Technologies, Inc. Publishing Division. Durham, North Carolina.

North American Projectile Point Identification Guides

Volume 1: North Carolina

Volume 2: Georgia

Volume 3: Florida

Volume 4: Alabama

Volume 5: Mississippi

Volume 6: Louisiana

Acknowledgements

This project involved far more time than I had anticipated. A very special thanks goes out to those colleagues who provided sources that were either exceedingly rare or saved me a large amount to time. In particular, I would like to thank:

The Louisiana Division of Archaeology for access to their site files, and providing such an easy system to use.

Anyone who paid money for this book. Those royalties help me buy the rare books and other sources I need to do the next state or province – I plan to do all of North America eventually.

Table of Contents

Why Use This Book? 7

About Using This Book..9

Quick Reference: Suggestions By Attribute..11

Louisiana Projectile Point Types:

Abasolo..13
Adena...14
Alba (Alba Barbed)..15
Almagre..17
Ashley..18
Bassett...19
Bayogoula (Bayou Goula)...20
Big Sandy..21
Bonham (Bonham Barbed)...22
Bulverde..23
Cache River..25
Carrollton Stemmed (Carrolton Stemmed)..26
Castroville...28
Catahoula..29
Cliffton (Cliffton Contracting Stem)..31
Clovis...32
Colbert...34
Collins Side Notched...35
Cuney..36
Dalton (Generic)..37
Delhi..39
Denton...41
Desmuke...42
Eden (Eden Yuma)...43
Edgewood...44
Edwards..45
Elam..46
Ellis..47
Ensor...49
Epps..51
Evans..52
Fresno...54
Friley...55
Frio..56

Gary	57
Godley	60
Hale	61
Hayes	62
Homan	63
Kent	64
Kirk Corner Notch	66
Kirk Serrated	68
Lange	69
Langtry	70
Ledbetter	71
Maçon	72
Marcos	74
Marshall	76
Martindale	78
Maud	79
Maybon (Mabin)	80
Meserve	81
Morhiss	82
Morrill Stemmed	83
Motley	84
Neches River	86
Nodena (Nodena Elliptical)	87
Nolan (Nolan Beveled)	88
Opossum Bayou	89
Palmer	90
Palmillas	92
Pelican	94
Perdiz (Foyle Flake)	95
Plainview	96
Pontchartrain	97
Reed	99
San Patrice	100
Scallorn Stemmed	102
Scottsbluff	104
Shumla	105
Sinner	106
St. Tammany	107
Trinity (Trinity Stemmed; Trinity Notched)	108
Webb	109
Wells	110
Williams	111
Woden	113
Yarbrough	114
Works Cited	116

Why Use This Book?

There are quite a few guides out there for identifying projectile points in North America. Unfortunately, they all suffer from some combination of the following limitations:

They cite unreliable sources

The most popular websites will list more than 200 types just for, say, the Carolinas region. This is driven by the fact that that amateur publications by various collector and hobbyist societies are cited on the same level as peer-reviewed articles and books. Peer review is not perfect, but it at least guarantees that someone will not simply name every point they pick up as a new type and then submit it to such avocational journals or ones that only peer review upon request.

While such publications are an important bridge between avocational archaeology participants, academic archaeologists, and private-sector archaeologists (cultural resource management), the proclamations of novel projectile point types only serve to add to the confusion around the myriad point types – and also to balloon the number of "rare and collectible" types.

Books, which tend to be more restrained if only due to printing cost, will suggest there are many thousands of identified types in North America. Unfortunately, even the ones that provide a little quality information either contain few citations or copious numbers of self-citations and non-scholarly sources. Upon close inspection, an astute reader will even find sources that both cite each other, whereupon it becomes difficult to determine exactly which party was the original reference.

Any projectile points included in this volume have firm academic consensus behind them. Many have been excluded because they are not professionally cited. Some of those types may make it into future editions of this volume. But only point types that are academically sourced and professionally used appear in this book at the moment.

Does that mean all of these points have perfect descriptions? Of course not. But it is the best that can be done for now. In nearly every case, descriptions are taken from the primary source. *The most important development that can happen in North American prehistoric archaeology is increased consistency of artifact classification.* Whenever possible, it is the original description that is referred to in the guides and other information within this series.

Uncertain intentions

Probably the most-purchased guide to projectile points is *The Official Overstreet Arrowheads Identification and Price Guide*. This is, of course, a book published by an artifact dealer. The entire business is to entice individuals to purchase artifacts from Overstreet. Not only is this a reprehensible encouragement for the illegal looting of our nation's cultural resources, but it also means there is an incentive to define point types in a way that maximize their collectability.

Never trust an artifact dealer for information about artifacts. The reader will find no mention of monetary value of artifacts in this book. Collecting and profiting are two very different past times – one is born from interest and the other from business interests.

Unclear geographic ranges

When first embarking upon the project to create guides for all of North America, it was simply to make a list of all the projectile points known within North Carolina. Unfortunately, even the simple task of building an exhaustive list of known point types within a single state is incredibly hard to do.

The decision was made early on to only include projectile points for a given state if there are at least two documented examples of that type within the scholarly archaeological literature. This generally means within an archaeology journal or scholarly book, though there is also much information available in reports made to state historic preservation offices by professional archaeological consultants.

If a point type appears in this work, there will be a primary source reference to that type and where in the state it was identified. This is not to be considered a completely exhaustive search of the state's archaeology, but merely that the point type in question does, indeed, appear in that state. The distribution maps do not account for density, as any density map would be wildly inaccurate owing to more archaeological work having been done in some counties than others.

About Using This Book

A total of 78 projectile point types were found to meet the following criteria for inclusion in this guide:

1) Type is described in a reliable, scholarly source (typically a peer-reviewed journal or a book published by a university or well-known academic press) and widely cited in other scholarly sources.
2) At least two specific examples of the type were identified within the borders of the state by a reliable, scholarly source – much of the geographic range data came from works put out by academic works, salvage archaeology operations, and the Louisiana State Historic Preservation Office.

The reader will find citations to primary sources and a brief overview of the point description. Note that some sources are no longer available in print, and are difficult to track down. This has led to discrepancies amongst other guides as to the definition of some types. Generally, the original descriptions are left to stand on their own merits unless there is an obvious error in the original source.

When the original source is not available, it is noted. In those few cases, the source that appeared to be most faithful to the lost original was used.

A range of reported examples is included, with a breakdown of citations by county. Generally, the bulk of these come from records at that state's historic preservation office, and are reported by professional CRM archaeologists. While collectors and avocational archaeologists can be a good source of extra information on a case-by-case basis, their data was not used in this volume unless reported to the state historic preservation office, due to the uncertain provenience and lack of professional, standardized documentation.

A silhouette of an "average" point of that type accompanies each written description. Generally, the example silhouette is of dimensions that fall in the middle of the accepted range, and whenever possible based heavily on the original examples. Full illustrations with flaking patterns have largely been excluded, as they tend to offer no better accuracy in identification to the average reader, but do offer a false sense of precision. The written description is probably far more helpful than pondering flaking or grinding patterns on a line and ink drawing.

A word of advice – the greatest weight of evidence in identifying a point should be placed on its base. The base is the least likely to have been reworked, and also has more features to work with that are likely functional – and thus be more consistent. Size should only be considered as a tiebreaker in many cases, and the author recommends only slight emphasis on the blade shape.

The very jargon of excurvate, incurvate, and recurvate are all suggestive of authors using obfuscatory language to make it sound important whether a blade edge is convex or concave. It seems likely that it is probably a matter of preference by the tool maker, and also a function of whether the point has been resharpened.

Even the best projectile point experts cannot identify all points. Cambron and Hulse, whose 1975 guide on Alabama projectile points was the model for this volume, would only classify around a quarter of the points at their disposal. If a point is being used to place a site's chronology, *it is better to simply acknowledge defeat than to put forth a spurious claim* that may simply be wishful thinking.

No judgement of the validity of point types included is generally made by the author. Projectile point typologies are at their core a modern way to classify artifacts that were handmade and unlikely to have followed a specific blueprint. These types are primarily useful for dating an archaeological deposit they are found in. Before ceramics become commonplace in the prehistoric chronology, lithic points are the primary means of dating most prehistoric sites in North America. They should not be mistaken for a cultural identity in most cases, despite there often being a case made exactly for that by some archaeologists.

Point typologies are tools for estimating age, and should not be assumed to do more.

Quick Reference: Suggestions By Attribute

Stemmed, Not Significantly Notched ("Christmas Tree"):
Adena
Alba (Alba Barbed)
Ashley
Bulverde
Carrollton Stemmed
Colbert
Denton
Edgewood
Elam
Gary
Hale
Hayes
Kent
Kirk Serrated Lange
Langtry
Ledbetter
Maçon
Maybon (Maybin)
Morhiss
Morrill Stemmed
Nolan (Nolan Beveled)
Pontchartrain
Scottsbluff
St. Tammany
Webb

Upward Barbs:
Friley

Triangles:
Fresno
Maud

Corner Notched:
Alba (Alba Barbed)
Ashley
Bonham (Bonham Barbed)
Castroville
Catahoula
Cuney
Delhi
Ellis
Ensor
Epps
Frio
Homan
Kirk Corner Notch
Marcos
Martindale
Motley
Neches River
Palmer
Palmillas
Scallorn Stemmed
Williams

Basal Notched:
Castroville
Marshall
Shumla

Fluted:
Clovis
Meserve
Pelican
San Patrice

Side Notched:
Big Sandy
Cache River
Castroville
Collins Side Notched
Dalton (Generic)
Eden (Eden Yuma)
Ensor
Epps
Godley
Homan
Opossum Bayou
Reed
Trinity (Trinity Stemmed/Notched)

Multiple Side Notched:
Evans
Sinner

Bifurcated Base ("Kidney Bean Base" or "Fishtail Base"):
Bayogoula (Bayou Goula)
Cuney
Edgewood
Edwards
Frio
Martindale
Maud

Pointed Base/Tapered Stem:
Almagre
Bassett
Cliffton (Cliffton Contracting Stem)
Gary
Hayes
Langtry
Maybon (Mabin)
Perdiz (Foyle Flake)
Wells

Eared ("Auriculate"):
Clovis
Dalton (Generic)
Maud
Meserve
Pelican
Plainview
San Patrice

Lanceolate ("Leaf Shaped"):
Abasolo
Clovis
Desmuke
Nodena (Nodena Elliptical)

Louisiana Projectile Point Types:

Abasolo:
"**Dimensions in cm:**
Length: 3.8-7.4 cm, average 5.3 cm
Width: 22.2-4.2 cm, average 2.9 cm
Thickness: 0.6-1.4 cm, average 1.1 cm

Abasolo points have the outline of a tear drop, with rounded bases, slightly convex sides, and tapering tips. The broadest portion of the projectile point is just above the base where it blends into the sides. The bases are often thinned...

These artifacts have been roughed out by percussion-flaking, which usually converges toward the center. A commonly expressed hypothesis is that Abasolos are projectile-point blanks, and this idea has some merit. Most of the edges near the tips display pressure-flaking scars, and over half of the complete specimens have been retouched in such a manner as to make the tips beveled in cross section. The basal sections of about a fourth of the specimens have been chipped by percussion, although the chipping was not pronounced, and all of these showed evidence of pressure-retouching." (MacNeish et al. 1967, p56)

Carpenter and Paquin generally put this point around 1500 BCE (Carpenter and Paquin 2010, p165). Suhm and Krieger give a beginning date range of between 5000 BCE and 3000 BCE, with the type surviving until 500 CE (Suhm and Krieger 1954, p400)

No type site is referenced by MacNeish, but were first identified in Tamaulipas, Mexico (MacNeish et al. 1967, p56).

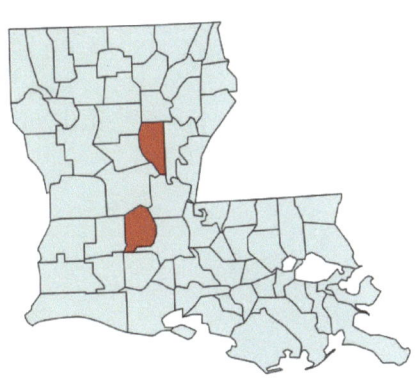

Reported Abasolo Specimens

These points have also been identified in:
Evangeline Parish (Louisiana Division of Archaeology 2020)
LaSalle Parish (Louisiana Division of Archaeology 2020)

Adena:
"Description: The Adena point is rather large in size with most examples ranging between 3 and 5 inches in length. The stem is broad, typically rounded and approximately semi-oval in outline. The shoulders are prominent but not barbed, and the blade edges form a gentle convex curve extending toward the tip. The Adena points are usually fairly thin, in spite of their width, and exhibit good workmanship in the chipping. In some cases the rounded stem has been ground or smoothed to dull the edges." (Bell 1958, p4)

Adena illustration from Cambron and Hulse 1975 (Public Domain)

The date range preferred by Justice and Kudlaty is 800-200 BCE (Justice and Kudlaty 1999, p36). Bell himself suggested a date range from 800 BCE to 800 CE based on radiocarbon dates from Prufer and Baby's work (Bell 1958, p4).

No type site is referenced by Bell, but it is named for the Adena culture with which it is associated (Bell 1958, p4).

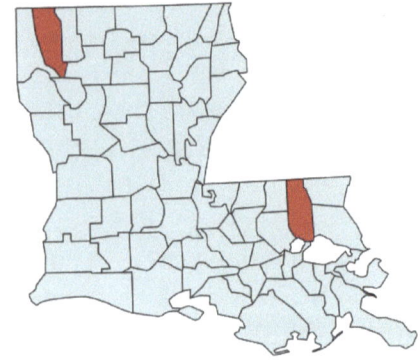

Reported Adena Specimens

These points have also been identified in:
Bossier Parish (Digital Index of North American Archaeology 2020)
Tangipahoa Parish (Digital Index of North American Archaeology 2020; Louisiana Division of Archaeology 2020)

Alba (also known as Alba Barbed in older publications):
"These have widely flaring barbs, blade edges usually concave, and the stem usually widest in the middle, giving it a bulb shape." (Krieger 1946, p115)

A most complete description was later given by Krieger in the famous <u>Introductory Handbook of Texas Archaeology</u>:

"**Outline:** Triangular blade with edges usually concave or recurved, seldom straight. Shoulders wide, outflaring, usually barbed. Stem edges usually parallel, occasionally contracted or expanded slightly. Base straight or slightly convex. Blade edges sometimes finely serrated.

Dimensions: Total length 1.8 to 3.5 cm. Maximum width quite uniform at about 1.5 cm, seldom more or less. Stem length about .7 cm on average, or ¼ to 1/5 total length." (Suhm and Krieger 1954, p494)

Suhm and Krieger assign a date range of 0-1200 CE with the possibility of later examples (Suhm and Krieger 1954, p494). Bell proposes a range of 700-1400 CE based upon several radiocarbon dates from the Harlan Site (Bell 1958, p8). Webb proposes a similar range of 750-1100 CE (Webb 1981, p14). Justice and Kudlaty give a date range of 900-1050 CE (Justice and Kudlaty 1999, p44).

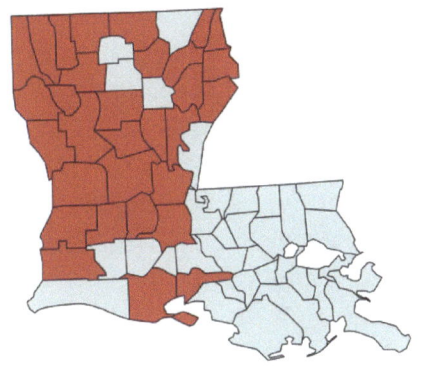

Reported Alba Specimens

No type site is referenced by Krieger.

<u>These points have also been identified in:</u>
Allen Parish (Louisiana Division of Archaeology 2020)
Avoyelles Parish (Louisiana Division of Archaeology 2020)
Beauregard Parish (Louisiana Division of Archaeology 2020)
Bienville Parish (Digital Index of North American Archaeology 2020; Louisiana Division of Archaeology 2020)
Bossier Parish (Louisiana Division of Archaeology 2020)
Caddo Parish (Digital Index of North American Archaeology 2020; Louisiana Division of Archaeology 2020; Webb and McKinney 1975, p95)
Calcasieu Parish (Louisiana Division of Archaeology 2020)
Catahoula Parish (Louisiana Division of Archaeology 2020)
Claiborne Parish (Digital Index of North American Archaeology 2020; Louisiana Division of Archaeology 2020)
DeSoto Parish (Louisiana Division of Archaeology 2020; Webb 1963, p179)
East Carroll Parish (Louisiana Division of Archaeology 2020)
Evangeline Parish (Louisiana Division of Archaeology 2020)
Franklin Parish (Louisiana Division of Archaeology 2020)

Grant Parish (Louisiana Division of Archaeology 2020)
Iberia Parish (Gagliano 1967, p85; Louisiana Division of Archaeology 2020)
LaSalle Parish (Digital Index of North American Archaeology 2020; Louisiana Division of Archaeology 2020)
Madison Parish (Louisiana Division of Archaeology 2020)
Natchitoches Parish (Louisiana Division of Archaeology 2020; Smith 1975, p184; Louisiana Division of Archaeology 2020)
Ouachita Parish (Louisiana Division of Archaeology 2020)
Rapides Parish (Louisiana Division of Archaeology 2020)
Red River Parish (Baker and Webb 1977, p245; Louisiana Division of Archaeology 2020; Webb 1948b, p135; Wright 1980, p219)
Richland Parish (Louisiana Division of Archaeology 2020; Penvy 2014, p4)
Sabine Parish (Louisiana Division of Archaeology 2020)
St. Landry Parish (Louisiana Division of Archaeology 2020)
Tensas Parish (Louisiana Division of Archaeology 2020)
Union Parish (Digital Index of North American Archaeology 2020)
Vermilion Parish (Louisiana Division of Archaeology 2020)
Vernon Parish (Anderson and Smith 2003, p243; Digital Index of North American Archaeology 2020; Louisiana Division of Archaeology 2020)
Webster Parish (Digital Index of North American Archaeology 2020; Louisiana Division of Archaeology 2020)
West Carroll Parish (Ford and Webb 1956, p69)
Winn Parish (Digital Index of North American Archaeology 2020; Louisiana Division of Archaeology 2020)

Almagre:
"Dimensions in cm:
Length: 4.7 to over 5.7 cm, average 5.1 cm
Width: 3.1-4.3 cm, average 3.6 cm
Thickness: 0.4-1.1 cm, average 0.6 cm
Stem Length: 0.3-1.6 cm, average 0.8 cm
Stem Width: 1.3-3.0 cm, average 2.0 cm

These projectile points have wide, triangular bodies and poorly defined, short, wide, convex to pointed stems. In many cases the stem is little more than a 'bump' in the middles of the base. Almagre points are made of thin, flat flakes which have a few percussion scars on their surfaces. These scars generally point toward the center of the body but they give the appearance of radiating away from the center. The edges are usually very neatly retouched bifacially." (MacNeish et al. 1967, p66)

MacNeish suggests an earliest date of 7000 BCE to 5500 BCE, without comment on their eventual disappearance (MacNeish et al. 1967, p66). Suhm and Krieger give a date range of 3000 BCE to 500 CE (Suhm and Krieger 1954, p396).

No type site is referenced by MacNeish, but were first identified in Tamaulipas, Mexico (MacNeish et al. 1967, p66).

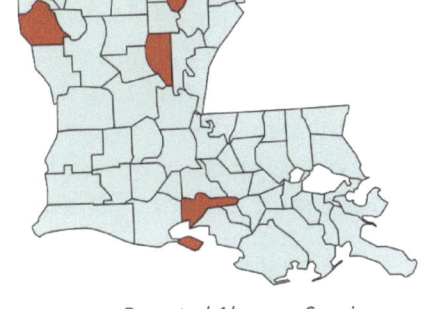

Reported Almagre Specimens

These points have also been identified in:
DeSoto Parish (Webb 1963, p177)
Iberia Parish (Gagliano 1967, p85)
LaSalle Parish (Louisiana Division of Archaeology 2020)
Richland Parish (Louisiana Division of Archaeology 2020)
West Carroll Parish (Ford and Webb 1956, p66)

Ashley:

"The blade is triangular with the edges usually concave or recurved although they are sometimes straight. The blade edges are sometimes finely serrated and the tips may be sharply incut. Generally, the points are bifacially chipped but some are unifacially chipped on a flake. The shoulders are wide and outflaring and usually slightly barbed although they are sometimes at right angles to the long axis of the blade. The barbs are pointed rather than broad. When the blade edges are recurved the lateral shoulders appear to be barbed. The stem is prominent and has a bulbous appearance with convex edges and base. It is this stem form that distinguishes this type from other types.

Dimensions:
The maximum length ranges from 21 to 28 mm and averages 25.1 mm. The maximum width of the shoulders ranges from 10 to 25 mm and averages 14.6 mm. The stem length ranges from 4 to 7 mm, averaging 5.8 mm. The stem is generally one-fourth the total length of the point. The stem width ranges from 7 to 11 mm, averaging 8.1 mm and is always wider than the stem length." (Rolingson 1971, p50)

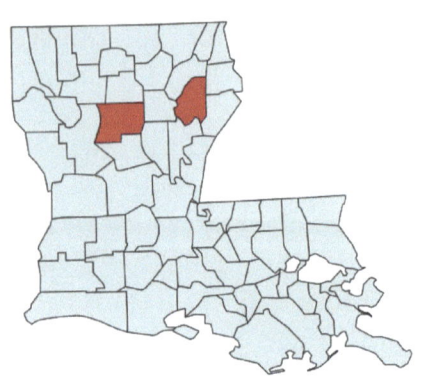

Reported Ashley Specimens

Rolingson suggests a date of 1100-1400 CE (Rolingson 1971, p50).

The type sites are in Bayou Bartholomew in Ashley and Chicot Counties, Arkansas (Rolingson 1971, p50).

These points have also been found in:
Franklin Parish (Louisiana Division of Archaeology 2020)
Winn Parish (Louisiana Division of Archaeology 2020)

Bassett:

Suhm and Krieger attribute these points to an unpublished note by Krieger and a 1948 article by Webb, but the first formal description comes from Suhm and Krieger's famous <u>Introductory Handbook of Texas Archaeology</u>:

"**Outline:** Very small triangular blades with edges usually straight, sometimes slightly convex or concave. Occasionally, tip is slimmed down to needle sharpness. Tiny pointed stem is about equal in size to the two barbs; when barbs are rather long, stem is like a tiny protrusion in middles of a deeply concave base. Very thin and finely chipped artifacts with exceedingly fine edge serration common.

Dimensions: Total length about 1.7 to 4.2 cm, but few more than 3.5 cm. Maximum width about 1.2 to 1.8 cm, seldom more or less. Stems 0.1 to 0.5 cm long, seldom more than 0.3 cm." (Suhm and Krieger 1954, p494)

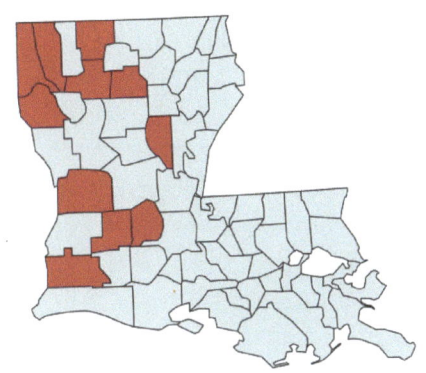

Reported Bassett Specimens

Suhm and Krieger propose a date range of 1200-1600 CE (Suhm and Krieger 1954, p494). Webb offers a similar range of 1200-1500 CE (Webb 1981, p15). Anderson and Smith largely concur with Webb's date of 1200 CE until the historic era (Anderson and Smith, p289).

No type site is referenced by Suhm and Krieger.

<u>These points have also been identified in:</u>
Allen Parish (Louisiana Division of Archaeology 2020)
Bienville Parish (Digital Index of North American Archaeology 2020; Louisiana Division of Archaeology 2020)
Bossier Parish (Digital Index of North American Archaeology 2020; Louisiana Division of Archaeology 2020)
Caddo Parish (Louisiana Division of Archaeology 2020; Webb 1948b, p132; Webb and McKinney 1975, p95)
Calcasieu Parish (Louisiana Division of Archaeology 2020)
Claiborne Parish (Louisiana Division of Archaeology 2020)
DeSoto Parish (Louisiana Division of Archaeology 2020)
Evangeline Parish (Louisiana Division of Archaeology 2020)
Jackson Parish (Louisiana Division of Archaeology 2020)
LaSalle Parish (Louisiana Division of Archaeology 2020)
Vernon Parish (Anderson and Smith 2003, p243; Digital Index of North American Archaeology 2020; Louisiana Division of Archaeology 2020)

Bayogoula (also known as Bayou Goula):
"...shaped somewhat like a swordfish; it has a tapered point which extends from a rounded body set on a fish-tail base. These projectile points are rather narrow in proportion to their length, then, and elliptical in cross section. They range in length from 28 to 52 mm and average about 3 mm in thickness. The chipping is rather fine and the execution is good. There were 26 points or fragments of this type excavated from the site, two of which had serrated edges." (Quimby 1957, p128)

These points are tentatively considered to be from the early historic period, based upon being found in burials with both European trade goods and ceramics such as Addis Plain, Fatherland Plain, and Neeley's Ferry Plain (Quimby 1957, p118). Webb states that these have been found with Alba, Catahoula, Hayes, and Colbert points, strongly suggesting contemporaneity (Webb 1981, p17). Anderson and Smith use a range of 1200-1500 CE (Anderson and Smith, p291).

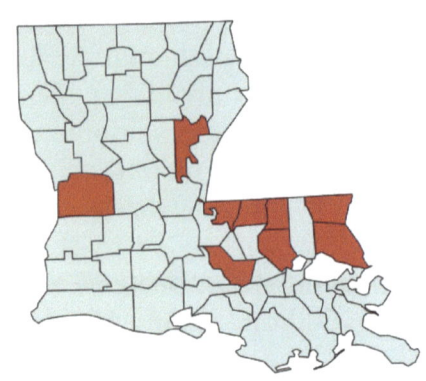

Reported Baygoula Specimens

The type site is the Bayou Goula Site in Iberville Parish, Louisiana (Quimby 1957, p128).

These points have also been identified in:
Catahoula Parish (Louisiana Division of Archaeology 2020)
East Feliciana Parish (Louisiana Division of Archaeology 2020)
Iberville Parish (Louisiana Division of Archaeology 2020; Quimby 1957, p128)
Livingston Parish (Louisiana Division of Archaeology 2020)
St. Helena Parish (Digital Index of North American Archaeology 2020; Louisiana Division of Archaeology 2020)
St. Tammany Parish (Louisiana Division of Archaeology 2020)
Vernon Parish (Anderson and Smith 2003, p243)
Washington Parish (Louisiana Division of Archaeology 2020)
West Feliciana Parish (Louisiana Division of Archaeology 2020)

Big Sandy:

"The basic shape is trianguloid, with excurvate side edges and incurvate or straight basal edge. The blade is usually thin and flat, and well retouched with pressure chipping. Rare examples show oblique, parallel chipping. The notches, which are perpendicular to the long axis of the blade, are usually narrow and short. The base is usually incurvate, either definitely or slightly. The portion of the blade between the notches and the base represents the unmodified basic shape of the blade before the notches were made." (Kneberg 1956, p25)

Big Sandy Illustration from Cambron and Hulse 1975 (Public Domain)

Kneberg noted these points were most common from 3500-1000 BCE (Kneberg 1956, p25). The points have also been found in association with very old types such as the Wheeler, Quad, and Dalton, and several radiocarbon dates at least as far back as 7000 BCE (Cambron and Hulse 1975, p14). Cambron and Hulse and Ritchie both believe this to be the same or closely related type as Otter Creek in New York (Cambron and Hulse 1975, p14; Ritchie 1971, p40). Justice and Kudlaty give a date range of 8000-6000 BCE (Justice and Kudlaty 1999, p16). Bell, gives a range of 5000-1200 BCE, noting that Big Sandy specimens become much more common around 3500 BCE (Bell 1960, p8).

The type site is the Big Sandy Site in Henry County, Tennessee (Kneberg, 1956, p25).

<u>These points have also been identified in:</u>
Lafayette Parish (Digital Index of North American Archaeology 2020)
Vernon Parish (Anderson and Smith 2003, p243)

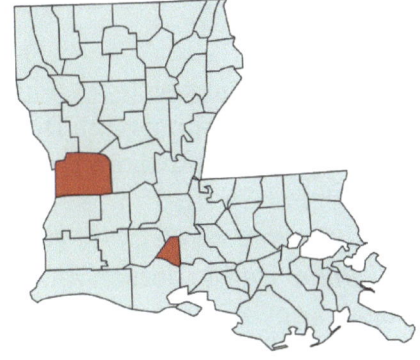

Reported Big Sandy Specimens

Bonham (also known as Bonham Barbed):
This type was first named but not described by Krieger in a 1946 publication. The first formal description comes from the famous <u>Introductory Handbook of Texas Archaeology</u>:

"**Description:** Slender triangular blade with edges usually straight but sometimes slightly concave or recurved; occasionally, slightly convex. Shoulders sometimes squared but usually have small barbs. Stem very narrow and parallel-edged. Base straight or slightly convex. Blade edges sometimes finely serrated.

Dimensions: Total length about 2 to 4 cm, occasionally 4.5 cm. Maximum width 1 to 1.5 cm, seldom as much as 2 cm. Stem length quite uniform at about 0.5 to 0.7 cm, 1/3 to 1/6 total length." (Suhm and Krieger 1954, p496)

Suhm and Krieger give a date range of 800-1200 CE (Suhm and Krieger 1954, p496). Webb suggests a range of 900-1200 CE (Webb 1981, p14).

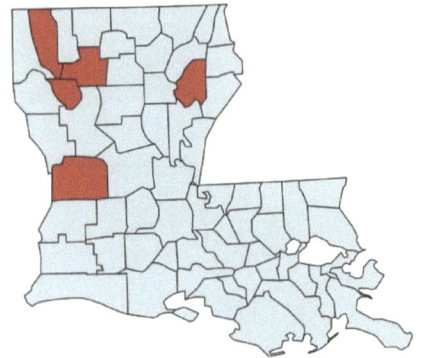

Reported Bonham Specimens

No type site is referenced by Suhm and Krieger.

These points have also been identified in:
Bienville Parish (Louisiana Division of Archaeology 2020)
Bossier Parish (Louisiana Division of Archaeology 2020)
Franklin Parish (Griffing 1985, p239; Louisiana Division of Archaeology 2020)
Red River Parish (Wright 1980, p220)
Vernon Parish (Anderson and Smith 2003, p243; Digital Index of North American Archaeology 2020)

Bulverde:
This type was originally identified, but not described, by Kelley in 1947. The first description was by Miller and Jelks in 1952:

"This type is distinguished by a straight base, square or slightly contracting stem, pronounced barbed shoulders, and a short, squat, triangular blade." (Miller and Jelks 1952, p176)

The first complete, detailed description comes from Suhm and Krieger:

"**Outline:** Blade usually triangular with straight to slightly convex edges, but occasionally strongly convex to leaf-shaped. Shoulders sometimes squared but usually have short barbs. In a few cases, barbs extend nearly to base of stem, possibly indicating separate type although barbs of all lengths form a continuous gradation around fairly uniform stem shape. Stem usually rectangular or slightly contracting and characterized by wedge shape; that is, from shoulder area, stem is thinned evenly to very sharp edge at base, with stem edges finely chipped. Base usually straight, may be very slightly concave or convex.

Dimensions: Total length ranges from about 4.5 to 9 cm, average about 6 cm. Stem usually 1/3 to ¼ total length. Stem width fairly uniform at 1.5 to 2 cm." (Suhm and Krieger 1954, p404)

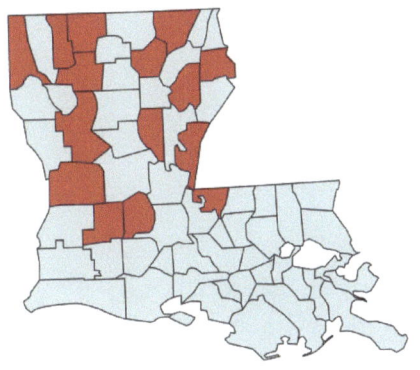

Reported Bulverde Specimens

Suhm and Krieger offer an age of 3000 BCE to 1000 CE (Suhm and Krieger 1954, p404). Anderson and Smith support a date range of 3700-3100 BCE based on data in Texas (Anderson and Smith 2003, p250).

The type site is the Lehmann Rock Shelter in Gillespie County, Texas (Kelley 1947, p124).

These points have also been identified in:
Allen Parish (Louisiana Division of Archaeology 2020)
Bienville Parish (Louisiana Division of Archaeology 2020)
Bossier Parish (Louisiana Division of Archaeology 2020)
Caddo Parish (Louisiana Division of Archaeology 2020)
Claiborne Parish (Digital Index of North American Archaeology 2020; Louisiana Division of Archaeology 2020)
Concordia Parish (Louisiana Division of Archaeology 2020)
Evangeline Parish (Louisiana Division of Archaeology 2020)
Franklin Parish (Griffing 1985, p239; Louisiana Division of Archaeology 2020)
LaSalle Parish (Louisiana Division of Archaeology 2020)
Madison Parish (Gregory et al. 1970, p42)
Morehouse Parish (Louisiana Division of Archaeology 2020)

Natchitoches Parish (Smith 1975, p184; Louisiana Division of Archaeology 2020)
Ouachita Parish (Louisiana Division of Archaeology 2020)
Vernon Parish (Anderson and Smith 2003, p243; Louisiana Division of Archaeology 2020)
Webster Parish (Louisiana Division of Archaeology 2020)
West Feliciana Parish (Louisiana Division of Archaeology 2020)

Cache River:
This type was first identified by Cloud in a 1969 avocational publication. The following description is by Perino:

"This is a thin, small to medium size dart point having narrow side notches. Exhibiting fine pressure flaking, they have a thin lenticular cross section. Bases are straight to slightly concave, and in most instances, lightly ground. They average 6 cm in length with narrow pressure-flaked notches occurring about 5 mm from the base. Notches may sometimes be expanded internally, and, on some examples, may enter the sides diagonally. Blades are thin and have convex edges and sharp tips." (Perino 1971, p14)

Geiger places these points as contemporary to San Patrice points, which he considers to be from around 8000 BCE (Geiger 1980, p17). Perino puts a similar date range, though mentioning that they may possibly precede San Patrice points (Perino 1971, p14).

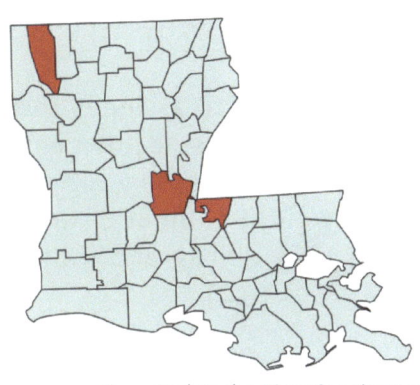

Reported Cache River Specimens

No type site is referenced, but the first identified examples were along the Cache River in Arkansas (Perino 1971, p14).

These points have also been identified in:
Avoyelles Parish (Louisiana Division of Archaeology 2020)
Bossier Parish (Louisiana Division of Archaeology 2020)
West Feliciana Parish (Louisiana Division of Archaeology 2020)

Carrollton Stemmed (also known as Carrolton Stemmed):
These points were first identified in 1952 by Crook and Harris, but were not described formally. The following description is from Suhm and Krieger's famous <u>Introductory Handbook of Texas Archaeology</u>:

"**Outline:** Triangular blade with prominent shoulders, squared or barbed; blade edges straight to slightly convex. Stem roughly rectangular, base straight to slightly convex. Stem edges, and sometimes base, commonly smoothed.

Dimensions: Total length ranges from about 3 to 6 cm, but shortest specimens probably reworked after tips shattered. Stem 1/3 to nearly ½ total length. Maximum width across shoulders 2.5 to 4 cm." (Suhm and Krieger 1954, p406)

Crook and Harris assigned the Carrollton Focus a date range equivalent to the Chiricahua, which they considered to be roughly 2000-1000 BCE (Crook and Harris 1952, p38). Bell agreed with this assessment (Bell 1958, p12).

The type sites are the Wheeler Site and Lake Dallas Site in Dallas County, Texas (Crook and Harris 1952, p12).

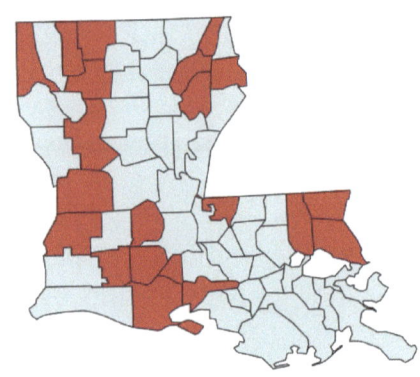

Reported Carrollton Stemmed Specimens

These points have also been identified in:
Acadia Parish (Louisiana Division of Archaeology 2020)
Beauregard Parish (Louisiana Division of Archaeology 2020)
Bienville Parish (Louisiana Division of Archaeology 2020)
Caddo Parish (Louisiana Division of Archaeology 2020; Neuman 1984, p84)
Claiborne Parish (Louisiana Division of Archaeology 2020)
DeSoto Parish (Louisiana Division of Archaeology 2020; Webb 1963, p177)
Evangeline Parish (Digital Index of North American Archaeology 2020; Louisiana Division of Archaeology 2020)
Franklin Parish (Griffing 1985, p239; Louisiana Division of Archaeology 2020))
Iberia Parish (Gagliano 1967, p85)
Jefferson Davis Parish (Louisiana Division of Archaeology 2020)
Lafayette Parish (Louisiana Division of Archaeology 2020)
Madison Parish (Louisiana Division of Archaeology 2020)
Natchitoches Parish (Louisiana Division of Archaeology 2020; Neuman 1984, p84; Smith 1975, p184)
Richland Parish (Louisiana Division of Archaeology 2020)
St. Tammany Parish (Digital Index of North American Archaeology 2020)
Tangipahoa Parish (Louisiana Division of Archaeology 2020)
Vermilion Parish (Louisiana Division of Archaeology 2020)
Vernon Parish (Anderson and Smith 2003, p243)

Washington Parish (Louisiana Division of Archaeology 2020)
Webster Parish (Louisiana Division of Archaeology 2020)
West Carroll Parish (Ford and Webb 1956, p55; Louisiana Division of Archaeology 2020)
West Feliciana Parish (Louisiana Division of Archaeology 2020)

Castroville:
The Castroville point was first named, but not described or illustrated, by Kelley in 1947. The first formal description was in Suhm and Krieger's famous <u>Introductory Handbook to Texas Archaeology:</u>

"**Outline:** Large triangular blade with edges often quite straight, but sometimes slightly convex, concave, or recurved. Shoulders occasionally small, but strong barbs common. Barbs grade from long, narrow to massive with tips in line with stem base. In latter cases, artifact probably blocked out first as large triangle with convex base, then notches cut inward from base. One barb often longer than other. Stems very broad and usually expand with rather straight edges; they may also be nearly parallel-edged. Bases straight to convex. The broad stems and general straightness of both stem and blade edges usually form an easily recognized combination.

Dimensions: Total length about 5 to 9 or 10 cm, average about 7 cm. Width across shoulders or barbs ranges from 3 to 6 cm. Maximum stem width ranges from 2.4 to 3.6 cm. Stem length usually ¼ to 1/3 total length." (Suhm and Krieger 1954, p408)

Suhm and Krieger suggest a date range of 4000 BCE to 1000 CE (Suhm and Krieger 1954, p408). Anderson and Smith cite more recent work that leads them to support a date range of roughly 950-360 BCE (Anderson and Smith 2003, p253).

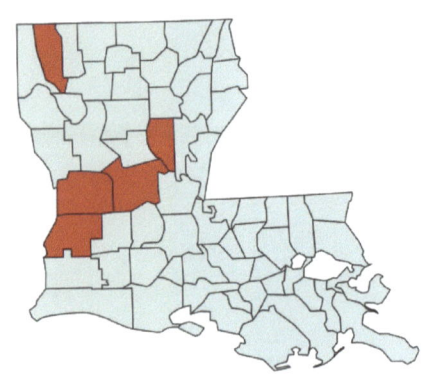

Reported Castroville Specimens

The type site is the Lehmann Rock Shelter in Gillespie County, Texas (Kelley 1947, p124).

<u>These points have also been identified in:</u>
Beauregard Parish (Louisiana Division of Archaeology 2020)
Bossier Parish (Louisiana Division of Archaeology 2020)
LaSalle Parish (Louisiana Division of Archaeology 2020)
Rapides Parish (Louisiana Division of Archaeology 2020)
Vernon Parish (Anderson and Smith 2003, p243)

Catahoula:
This type was first named in a 1956 publication by Webb and Gregory, but was formally described by Bell:

"The Catahoula point is an arrow point marked by distinctive barbs which produce a relatively broad shoulder area. The type is generally quite wide and flat, with good workmanship, and is perhaps somewhat larger than many other arrow point types. The blade edges are commonly recurved, often markedly concave, so that the blade appears short in reference to the broad shoulders.

The stem is short, wide, expanding and normally convex at the base. The notches are likely to be rather narrow and delimit a large and broad barb which is the most distinctive feature of this type. The broad barbs may be rounded or squared to form lateral projections and thus giving the maximum width of the point. The length ranges from ¾ inch to 1½ inches with some specimens being almost as wide as they are long." (Bell 1960, p16)

Baker and Webb give a date range of 800-1300 CE, based on a trio of radiocarbon dates and associations with Coles Creek, Plaquemine, and early Caddoan periods (Baker and Webb 1977, p249). Bell gives a date range of 1200-1600 CE based upon association with Plaquemine sites (Bell 1960, p16). Anderson and Smith give a range of 700-1100 CE (Anderson and Smith, p291).

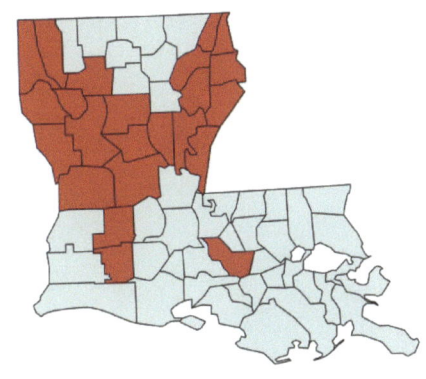

Reported Catahoula Specimens

The first examples were found near Catahoula Lake in Rapides and LaSalle Parishes, Louisiana (Bell 1960, p16).

These points have also been identified in:
Allen Parish (Louisiana Division of Archaeology 2020)
Bienville Parish (Baker and Webb 1977, p226; Louisiana Division of Archaeology 2020)
Bossier Parish (Baker and Webb 1977, p226; Louisiana Division of Archaeology 2020)
Caddo Parish (Baker and Webb 1977, p226; Webb and McKinney 1975, p95)
Catahoula Parish (Baker and Webb 1977, p226; Louisiana Division of Archaeology 2020)
Concordia Parish (Louisiana Division of Archaeology 2020)
DeSoto Parish (Baker and Webb 1977, p226; Digital Index of North American Archaeology 2020; Louisiana Division of Archaeology 2020; Webb 1963, p180)
East Carroll Parish (Louisiana Division of Archaeology 2020)
Franklin Parish (Louisiana Division of Archaeology 2020)
Grant Parish (Baker and Webb 1977, p226; Digital Index of North American Archaeology 2020; Louisiana Division of Archaeology 2020)
Iberville Parish (Baker and Webb 1977, p246)
Jefferson Davis Parish (Louisiana Division of Archaeology 2020)

LaSalle Parish (Louisiana Division of Archaeology 2020)
Madison Parish (Louisiana Division of Archaeology 2020)
Natchitoches Parish (Baker and Webb 1977, p226; Louisiana Division of Archaeology 2020)
Rapides Parish (Baker and Webb 1977, p226)
Red River Parish (Baker and Webb 1977, p226; Louisiana Division of Archaeology 2020)
Richland Parish (Louisiana Division of Archaeology 2020)
Sabine Parish (Louisiana Division of Archaeology 2020)
Tensas Parish (Louisiana Division of Archaeology 2020)
Vernon Parish (Anderson and Smith 2003, p243; Digital Index of North American Archaeology 2020)
West Carroll Parish (Ford and Webb 1956, p69; Louisiana Division of Archaeology 2020)
Winn Parish (Louisiana Division of Archaeology 2020)

Cliffton (also known as Cliffton Contracting Stem):
This type was first named by Krieger in a 1946 publication, but was first described in the famous <u>Introductory Handbook of Texas Archaeology</u>:

"**Outline:** Roughly triangular blade, crudely chipped, often modified on only one face, or on one face more than the other. Shoulders may project at right-angle but often are difficult to distinguish from the short, pointed stem. Blade edges may be fairly straight but often convex, concave, or asymmetrical.

Dimensions: Total length 2 to 4 cm. Maximum width about 1.5 to 2 cm, seldom more or less. Stem varies from barely visible to about 0.5 cm in length." (Suhm and Krieger 1954, p496)

Suhm and Krieger suggest a date range of 1200-1500 CE (Suhm and Krieger 1954, p496). Bell notes that it is found in the Washita River focus in Oklahoma archaeological sites (Bell 1960, p18). Anderson and Smith agree with Suhm and Krieger's date range (Anderson and Smith, p292).

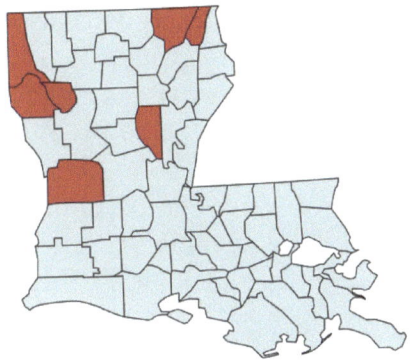

Reported Cliffton Specimens

No type site is referenced by Suhm and Krieger.

<u>These points have also been identified in:</u>
Caddo Parish (Louisiana Division of Archaeology 2020; Webb and McKinney 1975, p95)
DeSoto Parish (Webb 1963, p180)
LaSalle Parish (Louisiana Division of Archaeology 2020)
Morehouse Parish (Louisiana Division of Archaeology 2020)
Red River Parish (Wright 1980, p219)
Vernon Parish (Anderson and Smith 2003, p243; Louisiana Division of Archaeology 2020)
West Carroll Parish (Ford and Webb 1956, p69)

Clovis:

Howard spends a lengthy amount of time recounting his sources for description of Folsom points, and conservatively terms the points from Clovis as "Folsom-like" – which are the Clovis points archaeologists recognize today. He goes on to describe them as such:

"These 'Folsom-like' points are generally leaf-shaped with concave bases exhibiting a number of variations – some deeply concave, some shallow, and still others with a constriction just below the base forming a sort of 'fishtail'... Most of them are larger than the true Folsom point, heavier and thicker, and the secondary chipping is never as fine. The grooving is more apt to be irregular and to end more abruptly than on the Folsom point, characteristics that would be consistent with less well-controlled flaking as already pointed out. The use of the word 'groove' is not very exact. 'Fluting' or 'channeling' have been used to convey the same idea, but neither are any better, so we shall use 'groove.'" (Howard 1935, p110)

Clovis Illustration from Cambron and Hulse 1975 (Public Domain)

Most mainstream archaeologists would agree with radiocarbon dates associated with Clovis points that have variously suggested a lengthy range of use from around 9000 BCE (Ritchie 1971, p21) to around 7500 BCE (Cambron and Hulse 1975, p26). Boszhardt puts a relatively narrow range of 9300-8900 BCE on Clovis in the Upper Mississippi River Valley (Boszhardt 2003, p13). Justice and Kudlaty put a very widely accepted date range of 11000-9000 BCE (Justice and Kudlaty 1999, p2). Webb agrees with this range (Webb 1981, p2). How much earlier the Clovis occupation can be pushed back in various locations throughout North America is currently open to vigorous debate, but most archaeologists would agree Clovis is one of the oldest known projectile point styles in the New World.

The Blackwater Draw Locality Number 1 site in Roosevelt County, New Mexico is the type site (Howard 1935, p79).

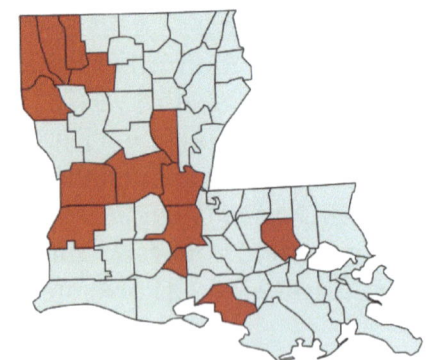

Reported Clovis Specimens

These points have also been identified in:
Avoyelles Parish (Louisiana Division of Archaeology 2020)
Beauregard Parish (Digital Index of North American Archaeology 2020; Louisiana Division of Archaeology 2020)
Bienville Parish (Webb 1948, p230)
Bossier Parish (Louisiana Division of Archaeology 2020)
Caddo Parish (Digital Index of North American Archaeology 2020; Louisiana Division of Archaeology 2020; Neuman 1984, p66)
DeSoto Parish (Louisiana Division of Archaeology 2020)

Lafayette Parish (Digital Index of North American Archaeology 2020; Louisiana Division of Archaeology 2020)
LaSalle Parish (Digital Index of North American Archaeology 2020)
Livingston Parish (Louisiana Division of Archaeology 2020)
Rapides Parish (Webb 1948, p230)
St. Landry Parish (Louisiana Division of Archaeology 2020)
St. Mary Parish (Louisiana Division of Archaeology 2020)
Vernon Parish (Anderson and Smith 2003, p243)
Webster Parish (Webb 1948, p230)

Colbert:
"...is characterized by expanded stems produced by corner notching, and blades which are much like Alba.

...The Colbert points have triangular blades with concave or recurved edges, distinct and usually wide shoulders, barbs, and triangular or fan-shaped stems. The stem bases may be straight or more often convex, rarely concave. Specimens from Smithport are made of tan, reddish-brown, white and gray local cherts, one of novaculite, and two of white quartz. Lengths are from 1.2 to 3.2 cm, widths from 9 mm to 2 cm." (Webb 1963, p180)

Anderson and Smith report an inferred date range of 850-1600 CE (Anderson and Smith 2003, p292). Webb himself later gave a range of 900-1100 CE (Webb 1981, p16).

The type site is the Smithport Landing Site in DeSoto Parish, Louisiana (Webb 1963, p180).

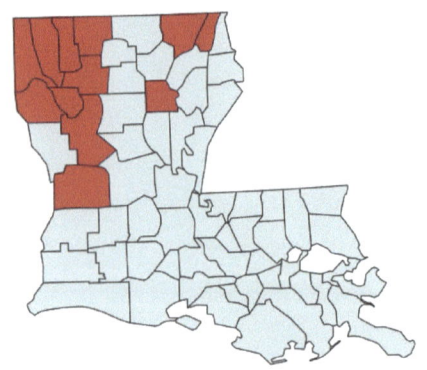

Reported Colbert Specimens

These points have also been identified in:
Bienville Parish (Louisiana Division of Archaeology 2020)
Bossier Parish (Louisiana Division of Archaeology 2020)
Caddo Parish (Webb and McKinney 1975, p95)
Caldwell Parish (Louisiana Division of Archaeology 2020)
Claiborne Parish (Louisiana Division of Archaeology 2020)
DeSoto Parish (Louisiana Division of Archaeology 2020; Webb 1963, p180)
Morehouse Parish (Louisiana Division of Archaeology 2020)
Natchitoches Parish (Louisiana Division of Archaeology 2020; Smith 1975, p184)
Red River Parish (Louisiana Division of Archaeology 2020)
Vernon Parish (Anderson and Smith 2003, p243; Digital Index of North American Archaeology 2020; Louisiana Division of Archaeology 2020)
Webster Parish (Louisiana Division of Archaeology 2020)
West Carroll Parish (Louisiana Division of Archaeology 2020)

Collins Side Notched:

"This type describes small, triangular, side-notched points with straight or excurvate blade edges. Point tips are characteristically attenuated beyond any functional requirements; in some cases, the blade edge even exhibits a visible recurve that draws finally to a delicate needle point at the very tip. This is one of the few types where fragments of the anterior end may be consistently classified. Basal edges are commonly straight but may be slightly convex or concave.

These points are characteristically well made; they are unusually thin, having an average thickness of only 4 mm, and are finely flaked (broad collateral removal) and retouched. In profile, the blade edges are straight or slightly excurvate, and the shoulders are prominent. Basal edges may be straight or curved.

Another diagnostic feature of these points is their size: they are at least 3.5 cm, and average 5 cm, in length. Regardless of length, width at the widest part of the blade is always in the very restricted range of 13 to 15 mm." (Williams and Brain 1983, 222-3)

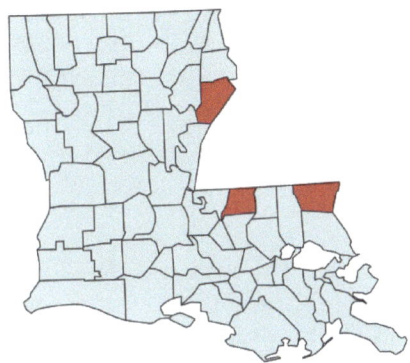

Reported Collins Side Notched Specimens

Williams and Brain note that this point type is strongly associated with the introduction of the bow and arrow and the Baytown period in Mississippi (Williams and Brain 1983, p223), by which they presumably mean around 500 CE, give or take several centuries.

The type site is the Lake George Site in Yazoo County, Mississippi (Williams and Brain 1983, 222).

These points have also been identified in:
East Feliciana Parish (Louisiana Division of Archaeology 2020)
Tensas Parish (Louisiana Division of Archaeology 2020)
Washington Parish (Louisiana Division of Archaeology 2020)

Cuney:
"**Outline:** Triangular blade with edges straight or concave and long barbs extending downward or flaring outward. Stem parallel-edges or slightly expanded. Base concave, from shallow curve to deep U-shaped notch.

Dimensions: Total length about 2 to 4.5 cm. Maximum width about 1 to 2 cm. Stems 0.4 to 0.7 cm wide and length about same. Stems from 1/3 to 1/6 total length." (Suhm and Krieger 1954, p498)

Suhm and Krieger offer a date range of 1600-1800 CE (Suhm and Krieger 1954, p498). Anderson and Smith infer a date range of 1200-1700 CE (Anderson and Smith, p293).

No type site is referenced by Suhm and Krieger.

These points have also been identified in:
LaSalle Parish (Louisiana Division of Archaeology 2020)
Rapides Parish (Louisiana Division of Archaeology 2020)
Sabine Parish (Digital Index of North American Archaeology 2020)
Vernon Parish (Anderson and Smith 2003, p243; Digital Index of North American Archaeology 2020; Louisiana Division of Archaeology 2020)
West Feliciana Parish (Louisiana Division of Archaeology 2020)

Reported Cuney Specimens

Dalton (generic):

"The most typical projectile points appear to be lanceolate blades with serrated edges and trianguloid points with concave base and serrated edges. Side-notched projectile points are also prevalent." (Chapman 1948, p138)

A more complete description can be found in many other volumes. Bell's 1958 work is the earliest useful, detailed description that could be found:

"Although it is not essentially a stemmed point, a stem or basal section is clearly marked off from the blade, either by grinding or a change in outline. The blade is triangular in outline, usually with straight or very slightly convex or concave edges. The stem or basal section is roughly parallel-sided; frequently slightly concave along the edges and terminated by a deeply concave base. The concave base is thinned by one or more relatively large flake scars on both faces. The sides of the base are ground or smoothed and this may extend across the concave base. The blade is well flaked to produce serrations, often forming a coarse saw-like edge. The blade, moreover, may be slightly or strongly beveled although strong bevels are more likely to occur on what appears to be resharpened specimens.

In size, the Dalton point rages from perhaps 1½ inches to 3 inches with most examples falling between 2 and 2½ inches in length." (Bell 1958, p18)

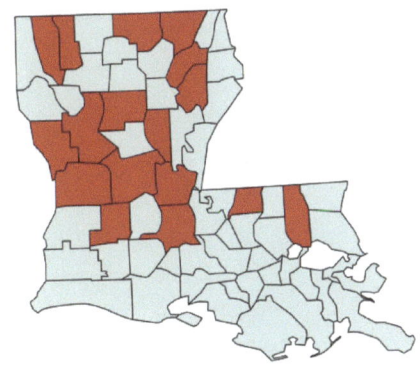

Reported Dalton Specimens

Geiger recommends a date of circa 8000 BCE (Geiger 1980, p17). Bell posits 8000-3000 BCE based upon stratigraphic evidence, especially at Graham Cave in Missouri (Bell 1958, p18). Justice and Kudlaty give a range of 8500-7900 BCE (Justice and Kudlaty 1999, p4). Boszhardt prefers a date range of 8000-6000 BCE (Boszhardt 2003, p31).

No type site is referenced by Chapman.

These points have also been identified in:
Allen Parish (Digital Index of North American Archaeology 2020; Louisiana Division of Archaeology 2020)
Avoyelles Parish (Louisiana Division of Archaeology 2020)
Beauregard Parish (Digital Index of North American Archaeology 2020)
Bossier Parish (Louisiana Division of Archaeology 2020)
East Feliciana Parish (Digital Index of North American Archaeology 2020; Louisiana Division of Archaeology 2020)
Franklin Parish (Digital Index of North American Archaeology 2020; Louisiana Division of Archaeology 2020)
LaSalle Parish (Louisiana Division of Archaeology 2020)

Morehouse Parish (Digital Index of North American Archaeology 2020)
Natchitoches Parish (Digital Index of North American Archaeology 2020)
Rapides Parish (Digital Index of North American Archaeology 2020; Louisiana Division of Archaeology 2020)
Richland Parish (Louisiana Division of Archaeology 2020)
Sabine Parish (Louisiana Division of Archaeology 2020)
St. Landry Parish (Louisiana Division of Archaeology 2020)
Tangipahoa Parish (Louisiana Division of Archaeology 2020)
Union Parish (Louisiana Division of Archaeology 2020)
Vernon Parish (Digital Index of North American Archaeology 2020; Guderjan and Morehead 1981, p10)
Webster Parish (Louisiana Division of Archaeology 2020)
Winn Parish (Louisiana Division of Archaeology 2020)

Delhi:

"The blades of Delhi points are long triangles – one third with straight sides and the majority with gently curving edges…

Rather wide corner notches are characteristic. These notches form barbs on the corners of the blade similar to, but slightly shorter than, the barbs of the Motley type. They never extend down even with the base of the stem. As a characteristic feature, stems are parallel-sided and nearly square. Most often, stem bases are straight with squared corners, less often slightly convex, rarely concave.

Delhi points are formed by the skillful detachment of large flakes so that the usual result is a thin, bifacially symmetrical blade with curving surfaces; only a few have perceptible central ridges… Usually blade edges are finished by delicate retouching, but only in two cases is this regular enough to resemble the ripple flaking of Pontchartrain.

On 80 points, the measured length ranges between 4.3 and 9 cm; 78 percent of these fall between 5 and 7.5 cm. Width ranges from 2.8 to 4.2 cm; average about 3.4 cm/ Uniformity of width is indicated by the fact that 80 percent fall between 3 and 4 cm in blade width. Thickness is between 5 and 12 mm; average 8 mm. Stem length averages 1.26 cm; width averages 1.53 cm; nearly half of the stems are square." (Ford and Webb 1956, p58-60).

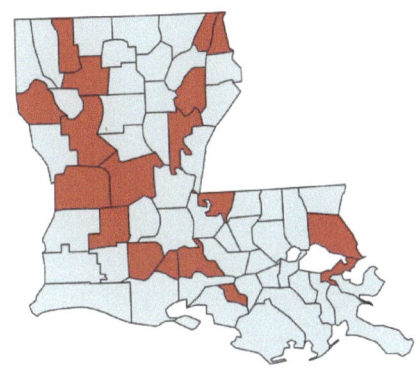

Reported Delhi Specimens

Justice and Kudlaty give a date range of 1300-900 BCE (Justice and Kudlaty 1999, p32). Ford and Webb generally put the Poverty Point site where they named this point in the late Archaic, from 1300-200 BCE, though they tentatively narrow it to 800-600 BCE (Ford and Webb 1956, p124).

The type site is Poverty Point in West Carroll Parish, Louisiana (Ford and Webb 1956, p58).

These points have also been identified in:
Acadia Parish (Louisiana Division of Archaeology 2020)
Allen Parish (Digital Index of North American Archaeology 2020; Louisiana Division of Archaeology 2020)
Bienville Parish (Louisiana Division of Archaeology 2020)
Catahoula Parish (Louisiana Division of Archaeology 2020)
DeSoto Parish (Louisiana Division of Archaeology 2020)
East Carroll Parish (Louisiana Division of Archaeology 2020)
Franklin Parish (Digital Index of North American Archaeology 2020; Griffing 1985, p239)
Lafayette Parish (Gibson 1979, p100)
Natchitoches Parish (Smith 1975, p184)

Orleans Parish (Shenkel 1974, p57)
Rapides Parish (Louisiana Division of Archaeology 2020)
St. Martin Parish (Louisiana Division of Archaeology 2020)
St. Tammany Parish (Digital Index of North American Archaeology 2020; Louisiana Division of Archaeology 2020)
Vernon Parish (Anderson and Smith 2003, p243; Digital Index of North American Archaeology 2020)
Webster Parish (Digital Index of North American Archaeology 2020; Louisiana Division of Archaeology 2020)
West Carroll Parish (Ford and Webb 1956, p58; Kuttruff 1975, p135; Louisiana Division of Archaeology 2020)
West Feliciana Parish (Louisiana Division of Archaeology 2020)

Denton:

"The Denton points are thick and crudely percussion flaked with a minimum of secondary chipping. Blade edges are sometimes straight, but usually slightly convex. Generally long, straight, and squared, or slightly expanded, the stem ranges from about one-fourth to one-third the length of the point, the latter proportion being quite common.

Bases are straight or slightly rounded and occasionally thinned. Shoulders vary from sloping to slightly barbed, but most examples slope somewhat.

Measurements for 96 Denton Site specimens are:
length – range 43-89 mm, average 67.5 mm;
width – range at shoulder 24-50 mm, average 33.4 mm;
thickness – range 9-17 mm, average 11.4 mm;
width – range at stem 16-30 mm, average 21 mm.

Most are made of local yellow, tan, or brown chert, but one is of novaculite, six are of Fort Payne chert, and three are of a material similar to Fort Payne. Most of this material was obtainable in local river gravels." (Connaway 1977, p24)

Reported Denton Specimens

Based on the limited radiocarbon evidence available to him, Connaway placed Denton points sometime prior to 3000 BCE (Connaway 1977, p28).

The type site is the Denton Site in Quitman County, Mississippi (Connaway 1977, p24).

These points have also been identified in:
Tangipahoa Parish (Digital Index of North American Archaeology 2020; Louisiana Division of Archaeology 2020)

Desmuke:

"**Outline:** Small, shoulderless, roughly lozenge-shaped points. Blade edges straight to convex; base contracts more or less to point rather than being convex to semicircular as in case of Abasolo points. Edges of base tend to be straight, or one edge fairly straight while other may be convex; base and blade frequently meet at a distinct angle. Blades sometimes beveled along either right or left each of both faces, but not as frequently as in Abasolo type.

Dimensions: Total length 3 to 5 cm, average about 4 cm. Maximum width 1.5 to 2.5 cm. Cross-section may be thick and diamond-shaped with ridge on each face." (Suhm and Krieger 1954, p416)

These points are not firmly dated, though Bell asserts that these are associated with pre-ceramic Archaic sites, at least in Oklahoma (Bell 1960, p30). Suhm and Krieger also generally assign Desmuke points to the Archaic (Suhm and Krieger 1954, p416).

No type site is referenced by Suhm and Krieger.

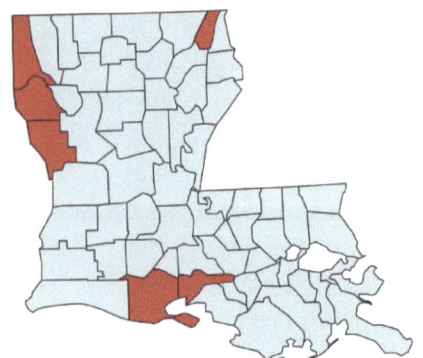

Reported Desmuke Specimens

These points have also been identified in:
Caddo Parish (Louisiana Division of Archaeology 2020)
DeSoto Parish (Webb 1963, p177)
Iberia Parish (Gagliano 1967, p85)
Sabine Parish (Louisiana Division of Archaeology 2020)
Vermilion Parish (Louisiana Division of Archaeology 2020)
West Carroll Parish (Ford and Webb 1956, p60)

Eden (also known as Eden Yuma in older publications):

"The most striking feature, next to the regular chipping with opposed scars, is the extreme narrowness with parallel edges. Examples are known with the width as little as one-seventh, or even one-eighth, of the length. The edges are parallel for two-thirds or even three-quarters of the total length. An Eden Yuma probably never widens above the base. They have notched-in stems, unlike any known fluted type. These notches are sometimes extremely shallow and seen only with close inspection, but there is no question that a stem was intended in most cases. The stem is thus only slightly narrower than the blade, its edges parallel and smoothed. The base is straight or slightly convex." (Krieger 1947b, p15)

Perino suggests these points were in use from an unknown period until around 5000 BCE, based on radiocarbon dates at the Horner Site (Perino 1971, p30). Boszhardt gives a range of 7200-6800 BCE specifically for the northern plains (Boszhardt 2003, p29). Justice and Kudlaty provide a date range of 6800-6400 BCE (Justice and Kudlaty 1999, p6).

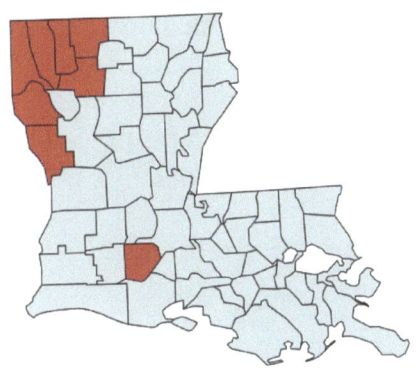

Reported Eden Specimens

The type site is near the town of Eden in Sweetwater County, Wyoming (Perino 1971, p30).

These points have also been identified in:
Acadia Parish (Digital Index of North American Archaeology 2020)
Bienville Parish (Webb 1948a, p230)
Bossier Parish (Webb 1948a, p230)
Caddo Parish (Webb 1948a, p230)
Claiborne Parish (Webb 1948a, p230)
DeSoto Parish (Webb 1948a, p230)
Sabine Parish (Webb 1948a, p230)
Webster Parish (Webb 1948a, p230)

Edgewood:

"**Outline:** Short triangular blade with edges sometimes straight, usually convex. Blade occasionally beveled on right edge of both faces. Shoulders prominent to well barbed. Stem edges expand widely with base often as wide as shoulders. Base may be nearly straight but is usually concave.

Dimensions: Total length about 3 to 5 cm, average about 4 cm. Maximum width 2 to 3 cm. Stem width usually 1.5 to 2 cm and stem usually 1/3 to ½ total length." (Suhm and Krieger 1954, p418)

Anderson and Smith infer an approximate date of 1000 BCE to 500 CE (Anderson and Smith 2003, p257). Suhm and Krieger simply state that these points are "probably late in Archaic" (Suhm and Krieger 1954, p418).

No type site is referenced by Suhm and Krieger.

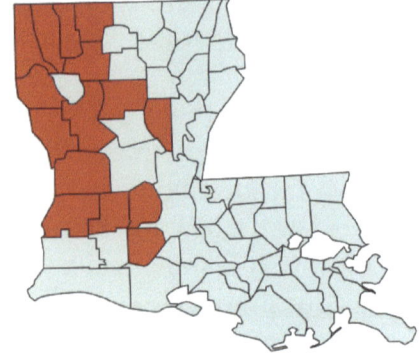

Reported Edgewood Specimens

These points have also been identified in:
Allen Parish (Louisiana Division of Archaeology 2020)
Beauregard Parish (Louisiana Division of Archaeology 2020)*Caddo Parish* (Louisiana Division of Archaeology 2020)
Caddo Parish (Louisiana Division of Archaeology 2020)
Evangeline Parish (Louisiana Division of Archaeology 2020)
LaSalle Parish (Louisiana Division of Archaeology 2020)
Natchitoches Parish (Digital Index of North American Archaeology 2020; Louisiana Division of Archaeology 2020)
Vernon Parish (Anderson and Smith 2003, p243; Guderjan and Morehead 1981, p10; Louisiana Division of Archaeology 2020)
Winn Parish (Digital Index of North American Archaeology 2020; Louisiana Division of Archaeology 2020)

Edwards:

"**Size:** Among the largest of arrow points. Maximum width varies from 1.4 cm to 2.3 cm. Length ranges from 2 cm to 4.5 cm with a large percentage about 4 cm long.

Blade: Triangular with straight to convex or slightly concave sides with frequent finely serrated edges, occasionally recurved; shoulders or barbs prominent and pointed, not squared.

Stem: Deeply divided into two long barb-like projections, each pointed, rounded, or squared, and leaving the long axis of the point at approximately 45 degrees or more, down and outward. On the bolder examples, these basal projections are narrow and curve either up or down." (Sollberger 1967, p14)

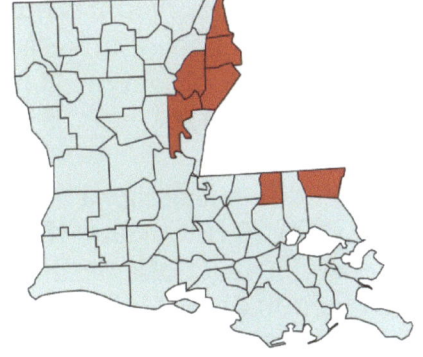

Perino points out that this point is found stratigraphically below Scallorn and Perdiz points (Perino 1968, p20).

The type site is in Kerr County, Texas (Sollberger 1967, p14).

Reported Edwards Specimens

These points have also been identified in:
Catahoula Parish (Louisiana Division of Archaeology 2020)
East Carroll Parish (Louisiana Division of Archaeology 2020)
Franklin Parish (Louisiana Division of Archaeology 2020)
Madison Parish (Louisiana Division of Archaeology 2020)
St. Helena Parish (Louisiana Division of Archaeology 2020)
Tensas Parish (Digital Index of North American Archaeology 2020)
Washington Parish (Louisiana Division of Archaeology 2020)

Elam:
These points were first named and photos published in a 1952 publication by Crook and Harris, but the first formal description coming from the famous <u>Introductory Handbook of Texas Archaeology:</u>

Outline: Small, stubby blade with edges straight to convex. Shoulders weakly developed to nearly absent. Stem roughly rectangular with edges parallel or slightly expanded or contracted, base straight to slightly convex. Stem edges often smoothed, base less often.

Dimensions: Total length of about 2 to 3.6 cm, average 2.5 to 3 cm. Stem usually about half the total length, sometimes little more or less. Small size may indicate use as arrow points, but thickness and workmanship compares with other dart-point types." (Suhm and Krieger 1954, p420)

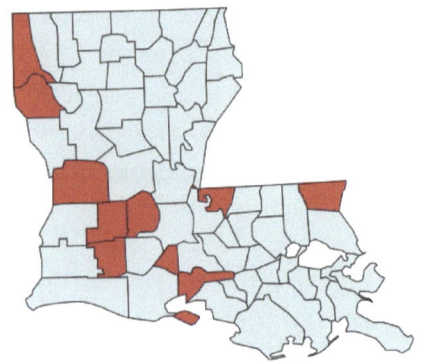

Reported Elam Specimens

Crook and Harris assign a date range of 500 BCE to 500 CE (Crook and Harris 1952, p12). Suhm and Krieger offer a slightly revised range of 500 CE to 450 CE (Suhm and Krieger 1954, p420).

The type sites are Wood and Milton Sites in northeast Texas near Dallas (Crook and Harris 1952, p27).

<u>These points have also been identified in:</u>
Allen Parish (Louisiana Division of Archaeology 2020)
Caddo Parish (Digital Index of North American Archaeology 2020; Louisiana Division of Archaeology 2020)
DeSoto Parish (Webb 1963, p177)
Evangeline Parish (Digital Index of North American Archaeology 2020; Louisiana Division of Archaeology 2020)
Iberia Parish (Gagliano 1967, p85)
Jefferson Davis Parish (Louisiana Division of Archaeology 2020)
Lafayette Parish (Gibson 1979, p100)
Vernon Parish (Anderson and Smith 2003, p243)
Washington Parish (Louisiana Division of Archaeology 2020)
West Feliciana Parish (Louisiana Division of Archaeology 2020)

Ellis:
First named by Newell and Krieger in a 1949 publication, it appeared also in Miller and Jelks' 1952 publication. The first detailed description comes in Suhm and Krieger's famous <u>Introductory Handbook of Texas Archaeology:</u>

"**Outline:** Short triangular blade with edges straight to convex, occasionally slightly concave. Shoulders prominent to well barbed. Stem expands toward base but never as broad as shoulders; stem edges tend to be straighter than in most types with cut-out corners. Bases straight to convex.

Dimensions: Total length about 3 to 5 cm. Maximum width across shoulders about 2 to 3 cm; smaller specimens may have been re-chipped. Stems equal ¼ to nearly ½ of total length and are 1/5 to 2 cm wide." (Suhm and Krieger 1954, p420).

Suhm and Krieger give a date range of 1000 BCE to 1000 CE (Suhm and Krieger 1954, p422). Webb gives a range of 2000 BCE to 600 CE (Webb 1981, p6). Anderson and Smith give a range of 1000 BCE to 500 CE (Anderson and Smith 2003, p259).

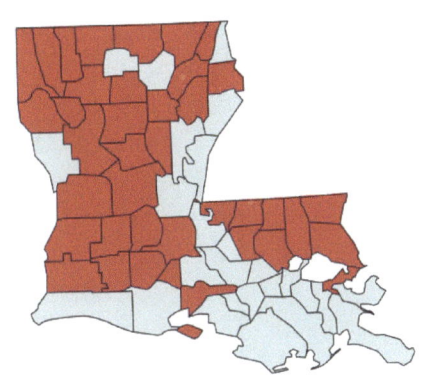

Reported Ellis Specimens

The type site is the George C. Davis Site in Cherokee County, Texas (Suhm and Krieger 1954, p422).

These points have also been identified in:
Acadia Parish (Louisiana Division of Archaeology 2020)
Allen Parish (Louisiana Division of Archaeology 2020)
Beauregard Parish (Digital Index of North American Archaeology 2020)
Bienville Parish (Louisiana Division of Archaeology 2020)
Bossier Parish (Digital Index of North American Archaeology 2020; Louisiana Division of Archaeology 2020)
Caddo Parish (Digital Index of North American Archaeology 2020; Louisiana Division of Archaeology 2020)
Calcasieu Parish (Digital Index of North American Archaeology 2020; Louisiana Division of Archaeology 2020)
Caldwell Parish (Louisiana Division of Archaeology 2020)
Claiborne Parish (Louisiana Division of Archaeology 2020)
DeSoto Parish (Louisiana Division of Archaeology 2020; Webb 1963, p177)
East Baton Rouge Parish (Digital Index of North American Archaeology 2020; Louisiana Division of Archaeology 2020)
East Feliciana Parish (Louisiana Division of Archaeology 2020)
Evangeline Parish (Digital Index of North American Archaeology 2020; Louisiana Division of Archaeology 2020)

Franklin Parish (Griffing 1985, p239; Louisiana Division of Archaeology 2020)
Grant Parish (Louisiana Division of Archaeology 2020)
Iberia Parish (Gagliano 1967, p85; Louisiana Division of Archaeology 2020)
Jackson Parish (Louisiana Division of Archaeology 2020)
Lafayette Parish (Gibson 1979, p100; Louisiana Division of Archaeology 2020)
LaSalle Parish (Hunter 1970, p84; Louisiana Division of Archaeology 2020)
Livingston Parish (Louisiana Division of Archaeology 2020)
Madison Parish (Gregory et al. 1970, p42)
Morehouse Parish (Louisiana Division of Archaeology 2020)
Natchitoches Parish (Louisiana Division of Archaeology 2020; Smith 1975, p184)
Orleans Parish (Shenkel 1974, p57; Shenkel and Holley 1974, p235)
Rapides Parish (Louisiana Division of Archaeology 2020)
Red River Parish (Louisiana Division of Archaeology 2020)
Richland Parish (Digital Index of North American Archaeology 2020; Louisiana Division of Archaeology 2020)
St. Helena Parish (Louisiana Division of Archaeology 2020)
St. Landry Parish (Louisiana Division of Archaeology 2020)
St. Tammany Parish (Digital Index of North American Archaeology 2020; Louisiana Division of Archaeology 2020)
Tangipahoa Parish (Louisiana Division of Archaeology 2020)
Union Parish (Digital Index of North American Archaeology 2020)
Vernon Parish (Anderson and Smith 2003, p243; Digital Index of North American Archaeology 2020; Guderjan and Morehead 1981, p13; Louisiana Division of Archaeology 2020)
Washington Parish (Louisiana Division of Archaeology 2020)
Webster Parish (Louisiana Division of Archaeology 2020)
West Carroll Parish (Digital Index of North American Archaeology 2020; Ford and Webb 1956, p55)
West Feliciana Parish (Louisiana Division of Archaeology 2020)
Winn Parish (Digital Index of North American Archaeology 2020; Louisiana Division of Archaeology 2020)

Ensor:
"The most prominent characteristic is a strongly expanding stem with a straight or convex base, the lateral extensions of the stem usually being approximately in line with the blade edges. Ensor resembles Ellis Stemmed, but differs from it in these respects: The expansion of the stem is sufficient to bring the stem corners flush with the blade edges, a small notch is frequently present in the middle of the base, markedly concave blade edges are common, the blade edges are sometimes serrated, and Ensor is generally longer, thinner, and of more slender proportions than Ellis." (Miller and Jelks 1952, p172)

Two years later, the Ensor points with concave bases were broken out into a separate type – the Frio type – with an updated description in Suhm and Krieger's famous <u>Introductory Handbook of Texas Archaeology</u>:

"**Outline:** Blade triangular and varying considerably in length and width; edges often quite straight, otherwise slightly convex, occasionally finely serrated. Shoulders vary from slight to pronounced; barbs, if present, are short. Stems very broad across the neck, due to notches being shallow, and bases commonly wider than shoulders so that basal corners are in line with blade edges. Occasionally base is less wide than shoulders but shallow notches and broad stem neck suggest Ensor type. Bases most commonly straight but may be concave.

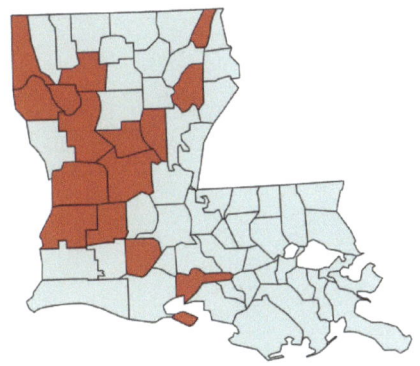

Reported Ensor Specimens

Dimensions: Total length about 3 to 7 cm, average perhaps 5 cm. Maximum width across base or shoulders from 2 to 3 cm. Stem seldom more than 1 cm long, therefore from 1/3 to 1/7 total length." (Suhm and Krieger 1954, p422)

Bell notes that in Oklahoma, these points are typically found on preceramic sites (Bell 1960, p34). Suhm and Krieger give a date range of 2000 BCE to 1000 CE (Suhm and Krieger 1954, p422). Anderson and Smith report a rough range of 4300 BCE to 200 CE, while acknowledging severe differences in dating examples in Louisiana compared to those in Texas (Anderson and Smith, p260).

The type site was part of the building of Belton Reservoir in Coryell County, Texas (Miller and Jelks 1952, p172).

<u>These points have also been identified in:</u>
Acadia Parish (Louisiana Division of Archaeology 2020)
Allen Parish (Louisiana Division of Archaeology 2020)
Beauregard Parish (Digital Index of North American Archaeology 2020; Louisiana Division

of Archaeology 2020)
Bienville Parish (Louisiana Division of Archaeology 2020)
Caddo Parish (Digital Index of North American Archaeology 2020; Louisiana Division of Archaeology 2020)
DeSoto Parish (Louisiana Division of Archaeology 2020; Webb 1963, p177)
Franklin Parish (Griffing 1985, p239; Louisiana Division of Archaeology 2020)
Grant Parish (Louisiana Division of Archaeology 2020)
Iberia Parish (Gagliano 1967, p85)
LaSalle Parish (Digital Index of North American Archaeology 2020; Hunter 1970, p84; Louisiana Division of Archaeology 2020))
Natchitoches Parish (Digital Index of North American Archaeology 2020; Neuman 1984, p84; Smith 1975, p184)
Rapides Parish (Louisiana Division of Archaeology 2020)
Red River Parish (Louisiana Division of Archaeology 2020)
Vernon Parish (Anderson and Smith 2003, p243; Guderjan and Morehead 1981, p13; Louisiana Division of Archaeology 2020)
West Carroll Parish (Ford and Webb 1956, p62; Kuttruff 1975, p135)

Epps:

"Epps are relatively narrow, triangular-bladed points with straight or, more commonly, slightly curved blade edges. Most... have lenticular profiles... Wide, deep notches into the corners and sides of these points produce roughly squared shoulders without barbs. These notches also leave flaring stems with rather narrow necks, but the stem bases are not as wide as the shoulders. The unusually narrow neck is a characteristic feature of the type.

The flaking, usually precise, produces fairly thin points, except on those that have median ridges. Some points are delicately retouched along the blade edges...

There is some variation in size. The lengths range from 3.7 to 8.2 cm; average, 5.1 cm. Widths range from 1.8 to 3.1 cm; average, 2.6 cm. Thickness is between 5 and 11 mm. The stems average about 15 mm in length; necks average 13 mm in width. From the neck the average point expands to a base that is about 18 mm wid. The stem is approximately one third of the total length in short points and one quarter of their total length in longer ones. Epps and Motley points have almost identical stems in both shape and size." (Ford and Webb 1956, p58)

Ford and Webb generally put the Poverty Point site where they named this point in the late Archaic, from 1300-200 BCE, though they tentatively narrow it to 800-600 BCE (Ford and Webb 1956, p124). Anderson and Smith include the Epps in a group of points they date to 4300 BCE to 200 CE (Anderson and Smith, p261).

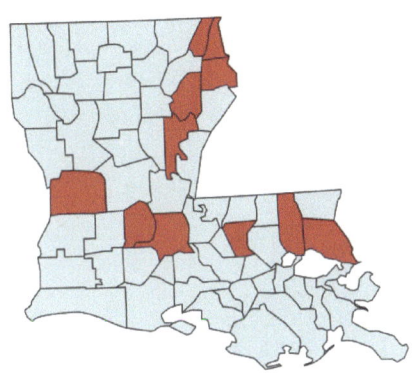

Reported Epps Specimens

The type site is Poverty Point in West Carroll Parish, Louisiana (Ford and Webb 1956, p58).

<u>These points have also been identified in:</u>
Catahoula Parish (Gibson 1975, p203; Louisiana Division of Archaeology 2020)
East Baton Rouge Parish (Louisiana Division of Archaeology 2020)
East Carroll Parish (Louisiana Division of Archaeology 2020)
Evangeline Parish (Louisiana Division of Archaeology 2020)
Franklin Parish (Griffing 1985, p239)
Madison Parish (Louisiana Division of Archaeology 2020)
St. Landry Parish (Louisiana Division of Archaeology 2020)
St. Tammany Parish (Louisiana Division of Archaeology 2020)
Tangipahoa Parish (Louisiana Division of Archaeology 2020)
Vernon Parish (Anderson and Smith 2003, p243; Digital Index of North American Archaeology 2020)
West Carroll Parish (Ford and Webb 1956, p58)

Evans:

Ford and Webb state that a more formal description would appear in a forthcoming publication, but none could be found amongst their subsequent publications.

"The specimens from Poverty Point have triangular blades with convex edges and well-defined square shoulders. Three stems expand slightly towards the base; the fourth contracts slightly.

The distinguishing feature of this type is the second set of notches worked into the blade edges a short distance above the shoulders. These notches are smaller than the corner notches, and the edges have not been blunted but remain rather sharp.

The primary shipping on these points is fairly good, resulting in rather thin blades, lenticular in coss-section. Blade edges have been straightened and sharpened by irregular delicate retouching.

Too few specimens are available to give complete size range. The smallest specimen is 5 cm long, 3.1 cm wide, and 6 mm thick. Two other specimens have about the same size and proportions. The largest measures 9.8 cm long, 3.7 cm wide, and 7 mm thick." (Ford and Webb 1956, p64)

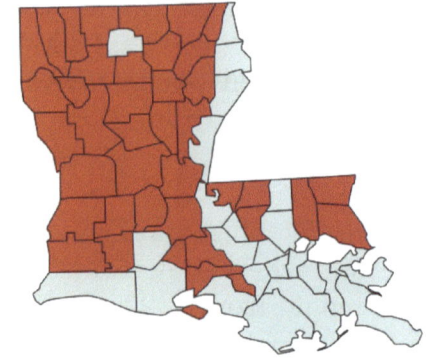

Reported Evans Specimens

Ford and Webb generally put the Poverty Point site where they named this point in the late Archaic, from 1300-200 BCE, though they tentatively narrow it to 800-600 BCE (Ford and Webb 1956, p124). Bell suggests that this type survived to more recent times, as it is associated with pottery at some Louisiana sites (Bell 1958, p24). Webb later gave a date range of 2500 BCE into the early Poverty Point era (Webb 1981, p10). Anderson and Smith include the Epps in a group of points they date to 4300 BCE to 200 CE (Anderson and Smith, p261).

The type site is Poverty Point in West Carroll Parish, Louisiana (Ford and Webb 1956, p64).

These points have also been identified in:
Allen Parish (Louisiana Division of Archaeology 2020)
Avoyelles Parish (Louisiana Division of Archaeology 2020)
Beauregard Parish (Louisiana Division of Archaeology 2020)
Bienville Parish (Louisiana Division of Archaeology 2020)
Bossier Parish (Digital Index of North American Archaeology 2020Louisiana Division of Archaeology 2020)
Caddo Parish (Louisiana Division of Archaeology 2020)
Calcasieu Parish (Louisiana Division of Archaeology 2020)
Caldwell Parish (Louisiana Division of Archaeology 2020)

Catahoula Parish (Louisiana Division of Archaeology 2020)
Claiborne Parish (Louisiana Division of Archaeology 2020)
DeSoto Parish (Louisiana Division of Archaeology 2020)
East Baton Rouge Parish (Gagliano 1963, p113)
East Feliciana Parish (Louisiana Division of Archaeology 2020)
Evangeline Parish (Louisiana Division of Archaeology 2020)
Franklin Parish (Louisiana Division of Archaeology 2020)
Grant Parish (Digital Index of North American Archaeology 2020; Louisiana Division of Archaeology 2020)
Iberia Parish (Gagliano 1967, p85)
Jackson Parish (Louisiana Division of Archaeology 2020)
Jefferson Davis Parish (Louisiana Division of Archaeology 2020)
Lafayette Parish (Gibson 1979, p100; Louisiana Division of Archaeology 2020)
LaSalle Parish (Digital Index of North American Archaeology 2020; Hunter 1970, p84; Louisiana Division of Archaeology 2020)
Morehouse Parish (Louisiana Division of Archaeology 2020)
Natchitoches Parish (Louisiana Division of Archaeology 2020)
Ouachita Parish (Louisiana Division of Archaeology 2020)
Rapides Parish (Louisiana Division of Archaeology 2020)
Red River Parish (Louisiana Division of Archaeology 2020)
Richland Parish (Louisiana Division of Archaeology 2020)
Sabine Parish (Louisiana Division of Archaeology 2020)
St. Landry Parish (Louisiana Division of Archaeology 2020)
St. Martin Parish (Louisiana Division of Archaeology 2020)
St. Tammany Parish (Louisiana Division of Archaeology 2020)
Tangipahoa Parish (Louisiana Division of Archaeology 2020)
Union Parish (Louisiana Division of Archaeology 2020)
Vernon Parish (Anderson and Smith 2003, p243; Louisiana Division of Archaeology 2020; Guderjan and Morehead 1981, p12)
Washington Parish (Louisiana Division of Archaeology 2020)
Webster Parish (Louisiana Division of Archaeology 2020)
West Carroll Parish (Ford and Webb 1956, p64; Louisiana Division of Archaeology 2020)
West Feliciana Parish (Louisiana Division of Archaeology 2020)
Winn Parish (Louisiana Division of Archaeology 2020)

Fresno:
This type was first named by Kelley in a 1947 publication, with the first formal description by Suhm and Krieger in the famous <u>Introductory Handbook of Texas Archaeology:</u>

"**Outline:** Simple triangles with straight to slightly convex edges, bases usually straight but may be concave or slightly convex. Usually finely flaked on both faces but occasionally one face is smooth fracture plan of original chip, only slightly modified if at all. Rarely, edges are finely serrated.

Dimensions: Length about 2 to 3.5 cm, seldom more or less. Width 1 to 2 cm, occasionally a little more." (Suhm and Krieger 1954, p498)

Suhm and Krieger put a date range of 800-1600 CE on Fresno points (Suhm and Krieger 1954, p498). These points are reported in Oklahoma as late as 1750 CE, eventually being replaced by metal points (Bell 1960, p44). Anderson and Smith offer a date range of 1200-1500 CE (Anderson and Smith, p293).

The type site is the Lehmann Rock Shelter in Gillespie County, Texas (Kelley 1947, p122).

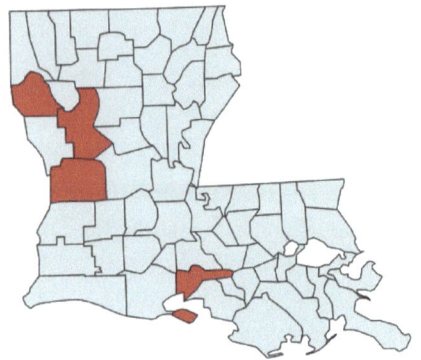

Reported Fresno Specimens

<u>These points have also been identified in:</u>
DeSoto Parish (Webb 1963, p181)
Iberia Parish (Gagliano 1967, p85)
Natchitoches Parish (Louisiana Division of Archaeology 2020; Smith 1975, p184)
Vernon Parish (Anderson and Smith 2003, p243)

Friley:
The Friley was first named by Webb, but the first description is from Bell:

"The Friley point is a small arrow point characterized by the unusual spurred shoulders. The points range in size from about ½ to 1½ inches. They are thin and rather well made in most examples. The diagnostic feature is the reversed shoulder or spurred shoulder projecting laterally or toward the tip. The stems are straight or slightly expanding with bases that are most commonly straight, but which may be slightly concave or convex." (Bell 1960, p46)

A date range of 700-1100 CE has been suggested by Anderson and Smith (Anderson and Smith 2003, p293).

The type site is the Friley Site in Louisiana (Bell 1960, p46).

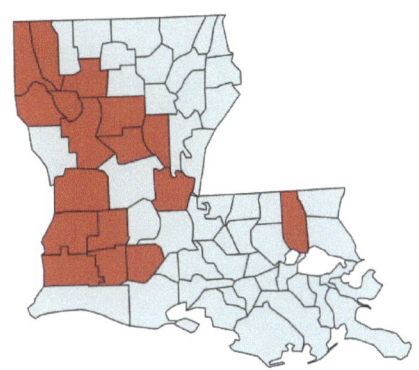

Reported Friley Specimens

These points have also been identified in:
Acadia Parish (Louisiana Division of Archaeology 2020)
Allen Parish (Louisiana Division of Archaeology 2020)
Avoyelles Parish (Louisiana Division of Archaeology 2020)
Beauregard Parish (Louisiana Division of Archaeology 2020)
Bienville Parish (Louisiana Division of Archaeology 2020)
Bossier Parish (Louisiana Division of Archaeology 2020)
Caddo Parish (Digital Index of North American Archaeology 2020; Louisiana Division of Archaeology 2020; Webb and McKinney 1975, p95)
Calcasieu Parish (Digital Index of North American Archaeology 2020; Louisiana Division of Archaeology 2020)
DeSoto Parish (Louisiana Division of Archaeology 2020; Webb 1963, p180)
Grant Parish (Louisiana Division of Archaeology 2020)
Jefferson Davis Parish (Louisiana Division of Archaeology 2020)
LaSalle Parish (Louisiana Division of Archaeology 2020)
Natchitoches Parish (Digital Index of North American Archaeology 2020; Louisiana Division of Archaeology 2020; Smith 1975, p184; Webb 1981, p16)
Red River Parish (Louisiana Division of Archaeology 2020; Wright 1980, p219)
Tangipahoa Parish (Louisiana Division of Archaeology 2020)
Vernon Parish (Anderson and Smith 2003, p243; Digital Index of North American Archaeology 2020; Louisiana Division of Archaeology 2020)
Winn Parish (Louisiana Division of Archaeology 2020)

Frio:
Outline: Triangular blade which is often short and broad, edges usually straight to convex but also fairly often concave or recurved. Shoulders occasionally weakly developed but usually strong or with good barbs. Stem formed by corner notches, often as wide as, or wider than, shoulders. Base always concave but in many cases recurved due to a deep U-shaped notch in center; in others, the notch is not prominent but the recurved basal edge suggests that it was chipped with this principal in mind.

Dimensions:
Total length about 3 to 7 cm, average perhaps 5 cm. Maximum width across shoulders or base 2 to 4 cm. Stem 1/3 to 1/6 of total length." (Suhm and Krieger 1954, p428)

Suhm and Krieger offer a date range of 3000 BCE to 500 CE (Suhm and Krieger, p428).

No type site is referenced by Suhm and Krieger.

These points have also been identified in:
Caddo Parish (Louisiana Division of Archaeology 2020)
Iberia Parish (Gagliano 1967, p85)
Natchitoches Parish (Smith 1975, p184)

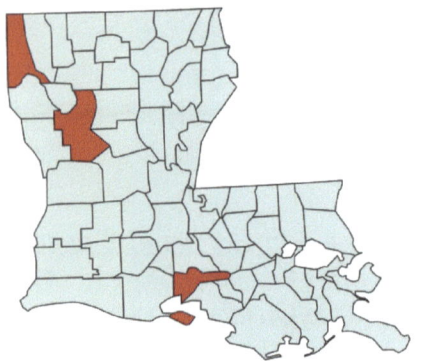

Reported Frio Specimens

Gary:

"**Outline:** Triangular blade with edges usually straight to convex but sometimes concave or recurved. Shoulders may be small but usually flare out widely almost at right angles; barbs, if present at all, are short. Stems usually contract strongly to pointed or somewhat rounded base but may at times approach being parallel-sided.

Dimensions: Total length about 4 to 8 cm, occasionally a little shorter or longer. Maximum width across shoulders 2 to 5 cm. Stems more constant in length than blades, so that on shorter specimens stem about ½ total length, on longer ones 1/3 to ¼." (Suhm and Krieger 1954, p430)

Suhm and Krieger give a date range of 2000 BCE to 1000 CE, noting a possibility of being as late as contact with Europeans (Suhm and Krieger 1954, p430). Cambron and Hulse excavated several in a late Archaic to Woodland context at the Stanfield-Worley Bluff Shelter (Cambron and Hulse 1975, p57). Justice and Kudlaty offer a slightly later date range from 1500 BCE with use continuing until 100 CE (Justice and Kudlaty 1999, p36). Webb gives a range of 2000 BCE to no later than 700 CE (Webb 1981, p8). Anderson and Smith prefer a range of 2500 BCE to 800 CE (Anderson and Smith, p265).

Gary illustration from Cambron and Hulse 1975 (Public Domain)

No type site is referenced by Suhm and Krieger.

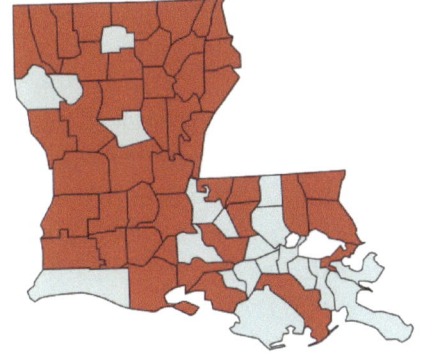

Reported Gary Specimens

These points have also been identified in:
Acadia Parish (Louisiana Division of Archaeology 2020)
Allen Parish (Louisiana Division of Archaeology 2020)
Avoyelles Parish (Digital Index of North American Archaeology 2020; Louisiana Division of Archaeology 2020)
Beauregard Parish (Digital Index of North American Archaeology 2020Louisiana Division of Archaeology 2020)
Bienville Parish (Louisiana Division of Archaeology 2020)
Bossier Parish (Digital Index of North American Archaeology 2020; Louisiana Division of Archaeology 2020)
Caddo Parish (Digital Index of North American Archaeology 2020; Louisiana Division of Archaeology 2020; Webb and McKinney 1975, p95)
Calcasieu Parish (Digital Index of North American Archaeology 2020; Louisiana Division of Archaeology 2020)
Caldwell Parish (Louisiana Division of Archaeology 2020)
Catahoula Parish (Digital Index of North American Archaeology 2020; Gibson 1975, p203; Hunter and Baker 1979, p43; Louisiana Division of Archaeology 2020)

Claiborne Parish (Louisiana Division of Archaeology 2020)
Concordia Parish (Digital Index of North American Archaeology 2020; Louisiana Division of Archaeology 2020)
DeSoto Parish (Digital Index of North American Archaeology 2020; Louisiana Division of Archaeology 2020; Webb 1963, p177)
East Baton Rouge Parish (Digital Index of North American Archaeology 2020; Gagliano 1963, p113; Louisiana Division of Archaeology 2020)
East Carroll Parish (Digital Index of North American Archaeology 2020; Louisiana Division of Archaeology 2020)
East Feliciana Parish (Digital Index of North American Archaeology 2020; Louisiana Division of Archaeology 2020)
Evangeline Parish (Louisiana Division of Archaeology 2020)
Franklin Parish (Digital Index of North American Archaeology 2020; Griffing 1985, p239; Louisiana Division of Archaeology 2020)
Iberia Parish (Gagliano 1967, p85; Louisiana Division of Archaeology 2020)
Iberville Parish (Louisiana Division of Archaeology 2020)
Jackson Parish (Digital Index of North American Archaeology 2020; Louisiana Division of Archaeology 2020)
Jefferson Davis Parish (Louisiana Division of Archaeology 2020)
Lafayette Parish (Gibson 1979, p100; Louisiana Division of Archaeology 2020)
Lafourche Parish (Louisiana Division of Archaeology 2020)
LaSalle Parish (Digital Index of North American Archaeology 2020; Hunter 1970, p84; Louisiana Division of Archaeology 2020)
Madison Parish (Gregory et al. 1970, p42; Louisiana Division of Archaeology 2020)
Morehouse Parish (Louisiana Division of Archaeology 2020)
Natchitoches Parish (Smith 1975, p184)
Orleans Parish (Shenkel 1974, p57; Shenkel and Holley 1974, p235)
Ouachita Parish (Digital Index of North American Archaeology 2020; Louisiana Division of Archaeology 2020)
Rapides Parish (Digital Index of North American Archaeology 2020; Louisiana Division of Archaeology 2020; Neuman 1984, p84)
Richland Parish (Lauro 2008, p87; Louisiana Division of Archaeology 2020)
Sabine Parish (Digital Index of North American Archaeology 2020; Louisiana Division of Archaeology 2020)
St. Landry Parish (Louisiana Division of Archaeology 2020)
St. Mary Parish (Digital Index of North American Archaeology 2020; Louisiana Division of Archaeology 2020)
St. Tammany Parish (Digital Index of North American Archaeology 2020; Louisiana Division of Archaeology 2020)
Tangipahoa Parish (Digital Index of North American Archaeology 2020; Louisiana Division of Archaeology 2020)
Tensas Parish (Digital Index of North American Archaeology 2020; Louisiana Division of Archaeology 2020)
Union Parish (Louisiana Division of Archaeology 2020)
Vermilion Parish (Digital Index of North American Archaeology 2020; Louisiana Division of Archaeology 2020)

Vernon Parish (Anderson and Smith 2003, p243; Digital Index of North American Archaeology 2020; Guderjan and Morehead 1981, p13; Louisiana Division of Archaeology 2020)
Washington Parish (Louisiana Division of Archaeology 2020)
Webster Parish (Digital Index of North American Archaeology 2020; Louisiana Division of Archaeology 2020)
West Carroll Parish (Ford and Webb 1956, p52; Kuttruff 1975, p135; Louisiana Division of Archaeology 2020)
West Feliciana Parish (Louisiana Division of Archaeology 2020)
Winn Parish (Louisiana Division of Archaeology 2020)

Godley:
NB: Jelks describes the main difference between Godley and Palmillas points as being the convexity of the stem edges. Based on examples given when both types are originally described, he appears to mean Godley points are concave from the point where the stem first meets the blade and then down to the corner of the base.

"**Overall Dimensions:** Length 4.0 to 6.0 cm; maximum width (at shoulders), 1.7 to 2.4 cm; maximum thickness, 5 to 7 mm.

Stem: The most characteristic attribute is a narrow, weakly expanding stem with a convex base. Length, 8 to 12 mm; maximum width (at base), 1.0 to 1.5 cm; maximum thickness, 3 to 5 mm.

Blade: Triangular with straight to somewhat convex edges. The shoulders are prominent but unbarbed.

Remarks: Godley points resemble Palmillas points but differ from Palmillas in having concave rather than convex stem edges." (Jelks 1962, p40)

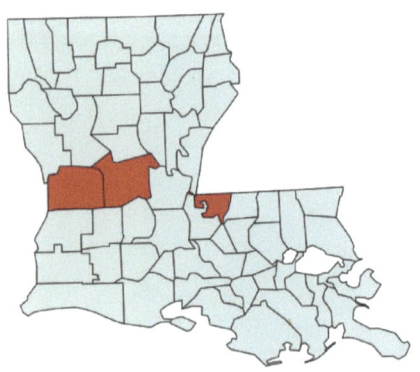

Reported Godley Specimens

Perino suggests a date range of 500 BCE to 500 CE (Perino 1968, p26). Anderson and Smith note a radiocarbon date associated with this type that was 136-462 CE (Anderson and Smith, p267), which is consistent with Perino's initial estimate.

The type site is the Kyle Site in Hill County, Texas (Jelks 1962, p40).

These points have also been identified in:
Rapides Parish (Louisiana Division of Archaeology 2020)
Vernon Parish (Anderson and Smith 2003, p243; Louisiana Division of Archaeology 2020)
West Feliciana Parish (Louisiana Division of Archaeology 2020)

Hale:

"Hale points are large, perhaps large enough to be classed as spear points rather than dart points. The blades are long triangles, with convex sides. The shoulders are square or slightly sloping; some points have very small barbs. Stems tend to be square or rectangular with parallel sides. Stem bases are straight, slightly concave, or slightly convex.

The primary shipping is generally quite competent. Irregularly shaped flake scars frequently run more than halfway across the faces of the blades. Blades are relatively thin and lenticular in cross section. The edges have been straightened and sharpened by irregular retouching. Most of the points are bifacially symmetrical…

Normally, Hale points range from 9.5 to 12 cm in length, from 3.5 to 5 cm in width, and from 15 to 22 cm in thickness. The stems are 13 to 20 mm long and 15 to 22 mm wide. Stems normally form from one fifth to one sixth of the point length." (Ford and Webb 1956, p64-5)

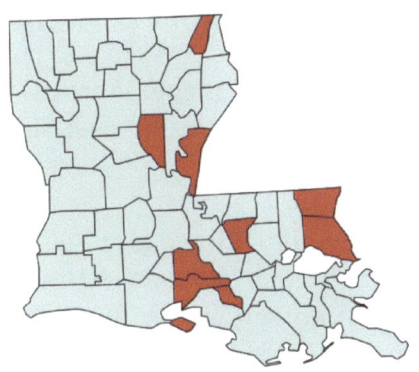

Reported Hale Specimens

Ford and Webb generally put the Poverty Point site where they named this point in the late Archaic, from 1300-200 BCE, though they tentatively narrow it to 800-600 BCE (Ford and Webb 1956, p124).

The type site is Poverty Point in West Carroll Parish, Louisiana (Ford and Webb 1956, p64).

These points have also been identified in:
Concordia Parish (Louisiana Division of Archaeology 2020)
East Baton Rouge Parish (Louisiana Division of Archaeology 2020)
Iberia Parish (Gagliano 1967, p85)
LaSalle Parish (Louisiana Division of Archaeology 2020)
St. Martin Parish (Louisiana Division of Archaeology 2020)
St. Tammany Parish (Digital Index of North American Archaeology 2020)
Washington Parish (Louisiana Division of Archaeology 2020)
West Carroll Parish (Ford and Webb 1956, p64)

Hayes:

"It resembles Alba Barbed but is longer and slimmer, and characterized by two special features: (1) a strong tendency to slim the tip to needle-like sharpness by exceedingly fine chipping; and (2) stems are characteristically diamond-shaped, often with tiny protrusions sticking out of the stem edges at odd angles." (Newell et al. 1949, p162)

Suhm and Krieger suggest a date range of 800-1200 CE, which is the same as the Haley Focus the type is associated with (Suhm and Krieger 1954, p502). Webb proposes a similar range of 800-1100 CE (Webb 1981, p15). Anderson and Smith provide an estimated range of 1000-1500 CE (Anderson and Smith, p294).

The type site is the George C. Davis Site in Cherokee County, Texas (Newell et al. 1949, p162).

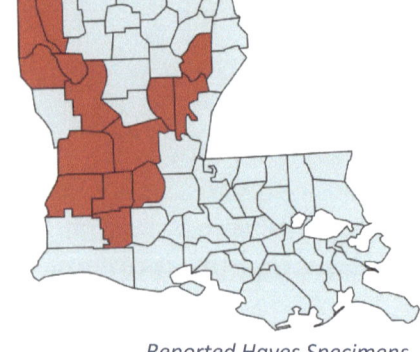

Reported Hayes Specimens

<u>These points have also been identified in:</u>
Allen Parish (Louisiana Division of Archaeology 2020)
Beauregard Parish (Louisiana Division of Archaeology 2020)
Bossier Parish (Louisiana Division of Archaeology 2020)
Caddo Parish (Digital Index of North American Archaeology 2020; Webb and McKinney 1975, p95)
Catahoula Parish (Louisiana Division of Archaeology 2020)
DeSoto Parish (Louisiana Division of Archaeology 2020; Webb 1963, p179)
Evangeline Parish (Louisiana Division of Archaeology 2020)
Franklin Parish (Louisiana Division of Archaeology 2020)
Jefferson Davis Parish (Louisiana Division of Archaeology 2020)
LaSalle Parish (Digital Index of North American Archaeology 2020)
Natchitoches Parish (Smith 1975, p184)
Rapides Parish (Louisiana Division of Archaeology 2020)
Red River Parish (Wright 1980, p219)
Sabine Parish (Louisiana Division of Archaeology 2020)
Vernon Parish (Anderson and Smith 2003, p243; Digital Index of North American Archaeology 2020)

Homan:

"**Form:** A small, base- or corner-notched arrow point.

Blade edges: Slightly recurved. They are generally convex near the tip, and concave above the shoulders; more rarely, gently convex to straight.

Notches: Deep and U- or V-shaped. Notches are directed into the blade between 45 and 90 degrees, creating a flared, fan-shaped stem.

Base: Evenly convex.

Flaking: They are pressure flaked, with random flake scars. Blade edges may be finely serrated. Bases are carefully thinned.

Dimensions: Length, 15 to 35 mm; maximum width (at shoulders), 8 to 18 mm; maximum thickness, 2 to 5 mm." (Wood 1963, p1)

Wood estimates a date range of 1000-1300 CE (Wood 1963, p2). Webb prefers a range of 800-900 CE (Webb 1981, p16).

The type sites are the Crenshaw Site in Miller County, Arkansas and the Poole Site in Garland County, Arkansas (Wood 1963, p1).

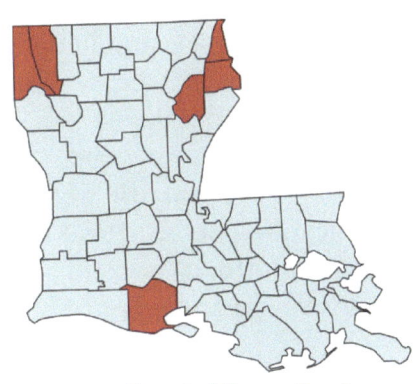

Reported Homan Specimens

These points have also been identified in:
Bossier Parish (Louisiana Division of Archaeology 2020)
Caddo Parish (Webb and McKinney 1975, p95)
East Carroll Parish (Louisiana Division of Archaeology 2020)
Franklin Parish (Griffing 1985, p239; Louisiana Division of Archaeology 2020)
Madison Parish (Louisiana Division of Archaeology 2020)
Vermilion Parish (Louisiana Division of Archaeology 2020)

Kent:
"**Outline:** Blade crudely triangular, often asymmetrical, edges usually convex but not in same degree; may be rather straight and in a few cases, concave. Shoulders weakly developed to right-angular; barbs uncommon and stronger on one side than other. Stems more or less parallel-edged, but like blades, usually poorly chipped and uneven. Bases usually convex, occasionally straight. Rarely, blade beveled.

Dimensions: Total length 3.5 to 7 cm, occasionally a little more or less, average about 4 to 5 cm. Maximum width across shoulders 1.5 to 3 cm. Stem 1/3 to 1/5 total length, 1 to 1.5 cm wide. Due to crude chipping, these specimens are usually notably thicker than other types. Those from central Texas are generally larger than those from coast." (Suhm and Krieger 1954, p432)

Suhm and Krieger simply date these points as "relatively late in Archaic Stage, in Christian era" (Suhm and Krieger 1954, p432). Bell more specifically suggests 1000 BCE to 1000 CE (Bell 1960, p60). Geiger suggests a late Archaic date (Geiger 1980, p19). Anderson and Smith offer a range of 500 BCE to 644 CE (Anderson and Smith, p268).

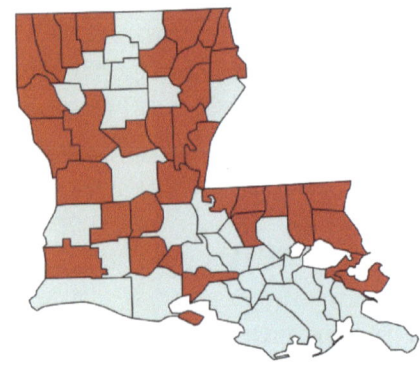

Reported Kent Specimens

No type site is referenced by Suhm and Krieger.

These points have also been identified in:
Acadia Parish (Louisiana Division of Archaeology 2020)
Allen Parish (Louisiana Division of Archaeology 2020)
Avoyelles Parish (Louisiana Division of Archaeology 2020)
Bossier Parish (Louisiana Division of Archaeology 2020)
Caddo Parish (Digital Index of North American Archaeology 2020; Louisiana Division of Archaeology 2020)
Calcasieu Parish (Digital Index of North American Archaeology 2020; Louisiana Division of Archaeology 2020)
Catahoula Parish (Gibson 1975, p203; Hunter and Baker 1979, p43; Louisiana Division of Archaeology 2020)
Claiborne Parish (Louisiana Division of Archaeology 2020)
Concordia Parish (Louisiana Division of Archaeology 2020)
DeSoto Parish (Louisiana Division of Archaeology 2020; Webb 1963, p177)
East Baton Rouge Parish (Digital Index of North American Archaeology 2020; Gagliano 1963, p113; Louisiana Division of Archaeology 2020)
East Carroll Parish (Louisiana Division of Archaeology 2020)
East Feliciana Parish (Digital Index of North American Archaeology 2020; Louisiana Division of Archaeology 2020)
Evangeline Parish (Digital Index of North American Archaeology 2020; Louisiana Division

of Archaeology 2020)
Franklin Parish (Digital Index of North American Archaeology 2020; Griffing 1985, p239; Louisiana Division of Archaeology 2020)
Grant Parish (Louisiana Division of Archaeology 2020)
Iberia Parish (Digital Index of North American Archaeology 2020; Gagliano 1967, p85; Louisiana Division of Archaeology 2020)
Lafayette Parish (Louisiana Division of Archaeology 2020)
LaSalle Parish (Digital Index of North American Archaeology 2020; Hunter 1970, p84; Louisiana Division of Archaeology 2020)
Madison Parish (Gregory et al. 1970, p42; Louisiana Division of Archaeology 2020)
Morehouse Parish (Digital Index of North American Archaeology 2020; Louisiana Division of Archaeology 2020)
Natchitoches Parish (Digital Index of North American Archaeology 2020; Smith 1975, p184)
Orleans Parish (Shenkel 1974, p57; Shenkel and Holley 1974, p235)
Ouachita Parish (Digital Index of North American Archaeology 2020)
Richland Parish (Louisiana Division of Archaeology 2020)
Sabine Parish (Louisiana Division of Archaeology 2020)
St. Bernard Parish (Digital Index of North American Archaeology 2020; Louisiana Division of Archaeology 2020)
St. Helena Parish (Louisiana Division of Archaeology 2020)
St. Tammany Parish (Louisiana Division of Archaeology 2020)
Tangipahoa Parish (Digital Index of North American Archaeology 2020; Louisiana Division of Archaeology 2020)
Vernon Parish (Anderson and Smith 2003, p243; Digital Index of North American Archaeology 2020; Guderjan and Morehead 1981, p13; Louisiana Division of Archaeology 2020)
Washington Parish (Louisiana Division of Archaeology 2020)
Webster Parish (Louisiana Division of Archaeology 2020)
West Carroll Parish (Ford and Webb 1956, p61; Louisiana Division of Archaeology 2020)
West Feliciana Parish (Louisiana Division of Archaeology 2020)

Kirk Corner Notch:
"A large triangular blade with a straight base, corner-notches, and serrated edges.

Form:
(1) Blade: Similar to Palmer Corner-Notched, but considerably larger. Edges were frequently serrated and occasionally beveled.
(2) Base: Generally straight or slightly rounded, but not ground or smoothed.

Size:
(1) Length: Range, 40 mm-100 mm; average, 60 mm.
(2) Width: Range, 20 mm-45 mm; average, 30 mm.
(3) Thickness: Range, 6 mm-12 mm; average, 8 mm.

Materials: Most specimens were made from argillite and novaculite. Igneous rocks were seldom used and quartz, not at all.

Technique of manufacture: The basic blade appeared to have been made with broad, shallow percussion flakes. The edges were then shaped by pressure flaking, and the serrations were made as a final step." (Coe 1964, p69-70)

Kirk Corner Notch Illustration from Cambron and Hulse 1975 (Public Domain)

Ward and Davis generally put Kirk types in the date range of 8000-6000 BCE (Ward and Davis 1999, p69). Cambron and Hulse report findings from Coe of a date around 6000 BCE (Cambron and Hulse 1975, p74). Broyles dated a hearth with specimens in Tennessee to about 7000 BCE (Broyles 1966, p19).

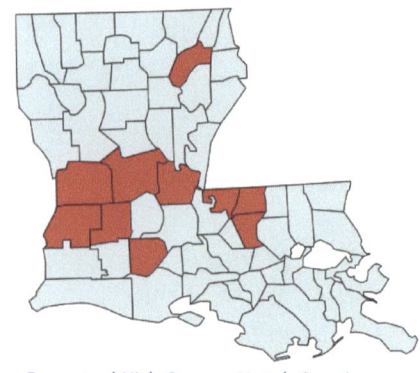

Reported Kirk Corner Notch Specimens

The type site is the Hardaway Site in Stanly County, North Carolina (Coe 1964, p70).

These points have also been identified in:
Acadia Parish (Louisiana Division of Archaeology 2020)
Allen Parish (Louisiana Division of Archaeology 2020)
Avoyelles Parish (Louisiana Division of Archaeology 2020)
Beauregard Parish (Digital Index of North American Archaeology 2020)
East Baton Rouge Parish (Gagliano 1963, p112)
East Feliciana Parish (Digital Index of North American Archaeology 2020)
Rapides Parish (Louisiana Division of Archaeology 2020)
Richland Parish (Digital Index of North American Archaeology 2020; Louisiana Division of Archaeology 2020)
Vernon Parish (Anderson and Smith 2003, p243; Digital Index of North American

Archaeology 2020)
West Feliciana Parish (Louisiana Division of Archaeology 2020)

Kirk Serrated:
"A long narrow blade with deep serrations and a broad square stem.

Form:
(1) Blade: Long, narrow, and relatively thick. The sides were always straight or nearly straight and deeply serrated. The short flake scars produced by the serrations again indicated that this was done after the basic blade had been shaped.
(2) Base: usually straight and blunt but occasionally thinned and concave... The base still shows the flat striking platform from which the original blade was struck.
(3) Stem: Always broad and nearly square. The width of the stem was usually about two-thirds of the width of the blade.
(4) Shoulders: Very narrow but squared with the stem.

Size:
(1) Length: Range, 45-120 mm; average, 70 mm.
(2) Width: Range, 25-35 mm; average, 30 mm.
(3) Thickness: Range, 8-12 mm; average, 9 mm.
Material: Same as for Kirk Corner-Notched.
Technique of manufacture: Same as for Kirk Corner-Notched." (Coe 1964, p70)

Kirk Serrated Illustration from Cambron and Hulse 1975 (Public Domain)

Ward and Davis generally put Kirk types in the date range of 8000-6000 BCE (Ward and Davis 1999, p69). Cambron and Hulse report findings from Coe of a date around 6000 BCE (Cambron and Hulse 1975, p74). Broyles dated a hearth with specimens in Tennessee to about 7000 BCE (Broyles 1966, p19).

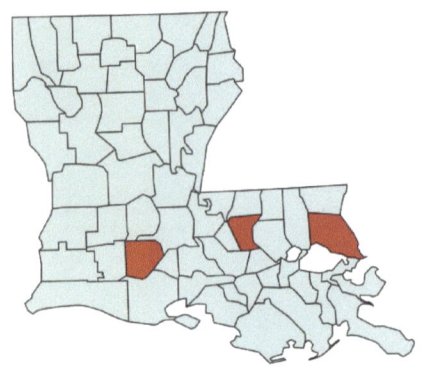

Reported Kirk Serrated Specimens

The type site is the Hardaway Site in Stanly County, North Carolina (Coe 1964, p70).

These points have also been identified in:
Acadia Parish (Louisiana Division of Archaeology 2020)
East Baton Rouge Parish (Louisiana Division of Archaeology 2020)
St. Tammany Parish (Digital Index of North American Archaeology 2020; Louisiana Division of Archaeology 2020)

Lange:
"**Outline:** Large triangular blade with edges straight to convex, occasionally concave or recurved. Shoulders prominent and often well barbed. Stem edges expand and are often straight, resembling those of Castroville type but not as wide. Base almost always straight but may be slightly concave or convex.

Dimensions: Total length about 5 to 8.5 cm. Maximum width across shoulders 2.7 to 4 cm. Stems 1.7 to 2.5 cm wide at bases and 1/3 to 1/5 total length." (Suhm and Krieger 1954, p436)

Suhm and Krieger propose a wide date range of 4000 BCE to 1000 CE (Suhm and Krieger 1954, p436). Bell asserts that this point is generally found in early Archaic horizons in Oklahoma (Bell 1958, p36). Anderson and Smith use a range of 850-600 BCE based on the Loma Sandia Site in Texas (Anderson and Smith, p268).

No type site is referenced by Suhm and Krieger.

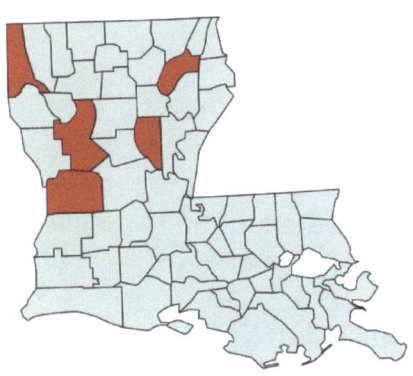

Reported Lange Specimens

These points have also been identified in:
Caddo Parish (Louisiana Division of Archaeology 2020)
LaSalle Parish (Louisiana Division of Archaeology 2020)
Natchitoches Parish (Louisiana Division of Archaeology 2020)
Richland Parish (Louisiana Division of Archaeology 2020)
Vernon Parish (Anderson and Smith 2003, p243; Guderjan and Morehead 1981, p12)

Langtry:
This type was first named by Kelley in a 1940 publication, with the first formal description by Suhm and Krieger in the famous <u>Introductory Handbook of Texas Archaeology:</u>

"**Outline:** Triangular blade with edges straight to concave or recurved, seldom convex, which is unique among Texas dart-point types. Usually exceedingly thin and finely chipped, even the largest ones. Shoulders prominent to widely outflaring, often uneven; barbs may sweep widely outward. Stems long, contracting, at times nearly parallel-edged or even expanding slightly. Bases are usually concave, even when stem contracts strongly, but may be straight or (rarely) convex…

Dimensions: Total length about 4 to 7 cm, average about 6 cm. Maximum width across shoulders about 2.2 to 4 cm. Base 0.6 to 1.6 cm wide. Stem often ½ total length but ranges to ¼." (Suhm and Krieger 1954, p438)

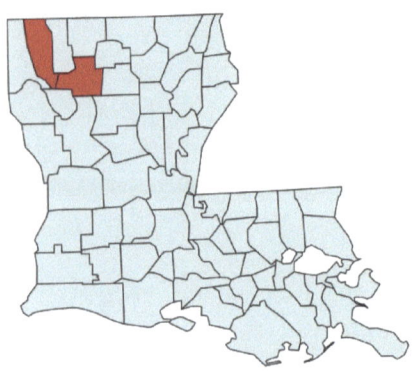
Reported Langtry Specimens

Suhm and Krieger put a date range with an unknown beginning to 800 CE (Suhm and Krieger 1954, p438). Bell reports this point being common on preceramic sites in Oklahoma, which suggests its use there at least as early as 0 CE (Bell 1958, p38).

No type site is referenced by Suhm and Krieger.

These points have also been identified in:
Bienville Parish (Louisiana Division of Archaeology 2020)
Bossier Parish (Louisiana Division of Archaeology 2020)

Ledbetter:

"The basic shape is trianguloid, and the distinctive feature of the blade portion is its asymmetry. The side edges are usually recurvate, but the recurvature is reversed on the two side edges. Thus, if one edge is excurvate-incurvated from the point to the shoulder, the other edge is incurvate-excurvate. This asymmetry of the edges results in the unequal shoulders that are diagnostic of the type. The incurvate-excurvate edge ends in a narrow, blunt shoulder, while the excurvate-incurvate edge ends in a flaring, barb-like shoulder. The stem is somewhat variable; it is usually straight or tapered with a straight basal edge, but it may be tapered with an excurvate basal edge. This latter variant is rare. The size is large with narrow breadth proportions, and the stem is relatively short." (Kneberg 1956, p26)

Ledbetter Illustration from Cambron and Hulse 1975 (Public Domain)

Kneberg suggests a date of 2000 BCE to "early centuries AD" (Kneberg 1956, p26). Justice and Kudlaty offer a date range of 2500-1000 BCE, though they as usual do not provide a reference, despite being recognized experts in the field of projectile points (Justice and Kudlaty 1999, p28).

The type site is the Ledbetter Site in Benton County, Tennessee (Kneberg 1956, p26).

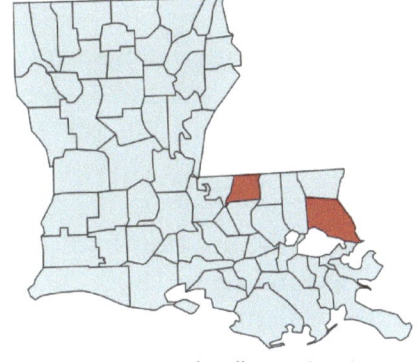

Reported Ledbetter Specimens

These points have also been identified in:
East Feliciana Parish (Digital Index of North American Archaeology 2020; Louisiana Division of Archaeology 2020)
St. Tammany Parish (Louisiana Division of Archaeology 2020)

Maçon (sometimes Macon in publications with limited printing ligatures):
"The points classed as Maçon are very similar to Gary, except that they have straight-sided rather than contracting stems. If these points were shorter, they might be classed as Carrollton. If the blades were barbed, they might be Delhi. If the blades were narrower and the flaking better, we might call them Pontchartrain...

...The blades of Maçon points are triangles that usually are about one and one-half times as long as they are wide at the shoulders. The blade edges are straight or slightly convex. The shoulders are square or very slightly sloping; none are barbed. Stems are straight-sided and range between one-fourth and one-fifth of the total length of the points. Stem bases are usually roughly squared, though some are slightly convex.

Large irregular flakes removed in the primary step of shaping the points produced low median ridges on the blade faces... Blade edges are usually finished by the removal of small irregular flakes.

Maçon points range in length from 5.5 to 7 cm; in width, from 2.8 to 3.7 cm; in thickness, from 8 to 12 mm. Stems average 1.43 cm in length and 1.57 cm in width. Materials are tan-brown, slate-gray, and dark brown chert."
(Ford and Webb 1956, p54)

Ford and Webb generally put the Poverty Point site where they named this point in the late Archaic, from 1300-200 BCE, though they tentatively narrow it to 800-600 BCE (Ford and Webb 1956, p124).

The type site is Poverty Point in West Carroll Parish, Louisiana (Ford and Webb 1956, p54).

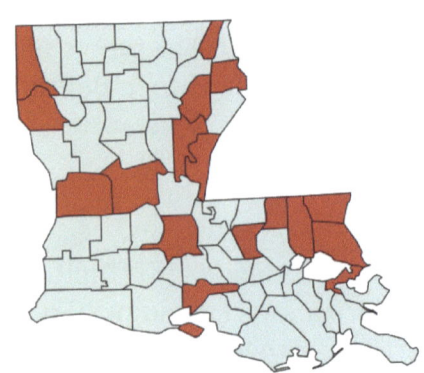

Reported Maçon Specimens

These points have also been identified in:
Caddo Parish (Louisiana Division of Archaeology 2020)
Catahoula Parish (Gibson 1975, p203; Louisiana Division of Archaeology 2020)
Concordia Parish (Louisiana Division of Archaeology 2020)
DeSoto Parish (Louisiana Division of Archaeology 2020)
East Baton Rouge Parish (Digital Index of North American Archaeology 2020; Louisiana Division of Archaeology 2020)
East Feliciana Parish (Louisiana Division of Archaeology 2020)
Franklin Parish (Griffing 1985, p239; Louisiana Division of Archaeology 2020)
Iberia Parish (Gagliano 1967, p85)
Madison Parish (Louisiana Division of Archaeology 2020)
Orleans Parish (Shenkel 1974, p57)
Rapides Parish (Neuman 1984, p84)
St. Helena Parish (Louisiana Division of Archaeology 2020)
St. Landry Parish (Louisiana Division of Archaeology 2020)

St. Tammany Parish (Digital Index of North American Archaeology 2020)
Tangipahoa Parish (Louisiana Division of Archaeology 2020)
Vernon Parish (Anderson and Smith 2003, p243; Louisiana Division of Archaeology 2020)
Washington Parish (Louisiana Division of Archaeology 2020)
West Carroll Parish (Ford and Webb 1956, p54)
West Feliciana Parish (Louisiana Division of Archaeology 2020)

Marcos:

"**Outline:** Generally broad triangular blade with edges straight, slightly convex, or gently recurved. Always barbed because deep notches cut into corners at about 45-degree angle; barb tips frequently in line with base. Angle of notches also always make stem strongly expanding; bases straight to convex, rarely slightly concave, generally not as wide as barbs.

Dimensions: Total length 4.5 to 9 or 10 cm, average 5 or 6 cm. Maximum width across barbs about 3 to 4.5 cm. Stem base about 2 to 3 cm wide and stem rather consistently about 1 cm long, thus 1/5 to 1/9 of total length." (Suhm and Krieger 1954, p442)

Suhm and Krieger give an age estimate of 2000 BCE to 1000 CE (Suhm and Krieger 1954, p442). Webb later gives a slightly shorter span of 2000 BCE to 500 CE (Webb 1981, p11). Anderson and Smith prefer a range of 1200 BCE to 634 CE (Anderson and Smith, p271).

No type site is referenced by Suhm and Krieger.

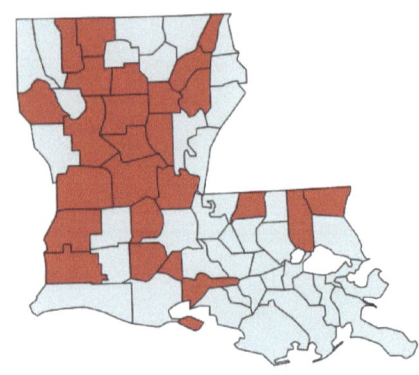

Reported Marcos Specimens

These points have also been identified in:
Acadia Parish (Louisiana Division of Archaeology 2020)
Avoyelles Parish (Louisiana Division of Archaeology 2020)
Beauregard Parish (Louisiana Division of Archaeology 2020)
Bienville Parish (Louisiana Division of Archaeology 2020)
Calcasieu Parish (Louisiana Division of Archaeology 2020)
Caldwell Parish (Digital Index of North American Archaeology 2020; Louisiana Division of Archaeology 2020)
Claiborne Parish (Louisiana Division of Archaeology 2020)
DeSoto Parish (Louisiana Division of Archaeology 2020)
East Feliciana Parish (Louisiana Division of Archaeology 2020)
Evangeline Parish (Louisiana Division of Archaeology 2020)
Franklin Parish (Griffing 1985, p239; Louisiana Division of Archaeology 2020)
Grant Parish (Digital Index of North American Archaeology 2020; Louisiana Division of Archaeology 2020)
Iberia Parish (Gagliano 1967, p85)
Jackson Parish (Louisiana Division of Archaeology 2020)
Lafayette Parish (Digital Index of North American Archaeology 2020)
LaSalle Parish (Louisiana Division of Archaeology 2020)
Natchitoches Parish (Digital Index of North American Archaeology 2020; Louisiana Division of Archaeology 2020; Neuman 1984, p84; Smith 1975, p184)
Rapides Parish (Digital Index of North American Archaeology 2020; Louisiana Division of Archaeology 2020)
Richland Parish (Louisiana Division of Archaeology 2020)

Tangipahoa Parish (Louisiana Division of Archaeology 2020)
Vernon Parish (Anderson and Smith 2003, p243; Digital Index of North American Archaeology 2020; Guderjan and Morehead 1981, p13; Louisiana Division of Archaeology 2020)
Washington Parish (Louisiana Division of Archaeology 2020)
Webster Parish (Digital Index of North American Archaeology 2020; Louisiana Division of Archaeology 2020)
West Carroll Parish (Ford and Webb 1956, p60; Kuttruff 1975, p135; Louisiana Division of Archaeology 2020)
Winn Parish (Digital Index of North American Archaeology 2020; Louisiana Division of Archaeology 2020)

Marshall:

Outline: Blade varies from triangular to broad oval, edges from nearly straight to greater part of a semicircle. Shoulders always strongly barbed, the more massive barbs commonly being in line with the base. Notches may have removed most of corner, but usually were cut upward into the blade from the base. Stem may be parallel-sided or slightly expanded, and is often quite short in proportion to the massive blade. Base straight or slightly concave or convex.

Dimensions: Total length about 5 to 11.5 cm, most between 6 and 8 cm. Maximum width about 3 to 5 cm, across barbs or middle of blade. Stems 1.2 to 2.5 cm wide and ¼ to 1/8 of total length." (Suhm and Krieger 1954, p444)

Suhm and Krieger give a range of 4000 BCE to 1000 CE (Suhm and Krieger 1954, p444). Bell notes that these points are commonly found with Pedernales points, implying that they are contemporaneous (Bell 1958, p44). Webb gives a date range of 3000 BCE to 500 CE (Webb 1981, p11).

No type site is referenced by Suhm and Krieger.

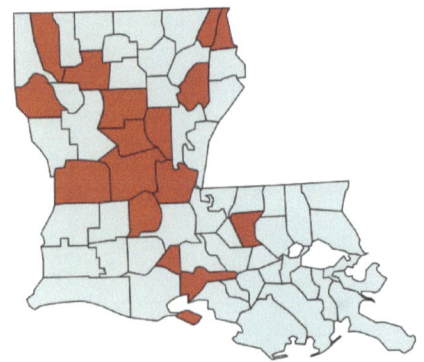

Reported Marshall Specimens

These points have also been identified in:
Avoyelles Parish (Louisiana Division of Archaeology 2020)
Bienville Parish (Louisiana Division of Archaeology 2020)*Claiborne Parish* (Louisiana Division of Archaeology 2020)
Bossier Parish (Digital Index of North American Archaeology 2020)
DeSoto Parish (Louisiana Division of Archaeology 2020)
East Baton Rouge Parish (Louisiana Division of Archaeology 2020)
East Carroll Parish (Louisiana Division of Archaeology 2020)
Evangeline Parish (Digital Index of North American Archaeology 2020; Louisiana Division of Archaeology 2020)
Franklin Parish (Digital Index of North American Archaeology 2020; Louisiana Division of Archaeology 2020)
Grant Parish (Louisiana Division of Archaeology 2020)
Iberia Parish (Gagliano 1967, p85)
Lafayette Parish (Gibson 1979, p100)
LaSalle Parish (Louisiana Division of Archaeology 2020)
Natchitoches Parish (Digital Index of North American Archaeology 2020; Neuman 1984, p84; Smith 1975, p184)
Rapides Parish (Neuman 1984, p84)
Vernon Parish (Anderson and Smith 2003, p243; Digital Index of North American Archaeology 2020; Louisiana Division of Archaeology 2020)

Winn Parish (Digital Index of North American Archaeology 2020)
West Carroll Parish (Ford and Webb 1956, p57; Kuttruff 1975, p135)

Martindale:
This type is first named by Miller and Jelks in a 1952 publication but was paired with an incorrect photo, and was formally described in the famous <u>Introductory Handbook of Texas Archaeology</u>:

"**Outline:** Triangular blade with edges sometimes straight, usually convex. Shoulders pronounced to well-barbed, but barbs seldom reach to base. Stem varies from nearly parallel-edged to strongly expanding. The most distinguishing feature of these points is that the base is formed by two distinct convex curves meeting in a depression in the center, a 'fish-tail…'

…On other specimens the base appears to be a simple recurve but close examination shows the double-convex 'fish-tail.' It is assumed that this form of base was the result of deliberate effort setting it apart from other bases.

Dimensions: Total length 3.5 to 7 cm, average 4 to 5 cm. Maximum width across shoulders 2.5 to 4.5 cm. Stems 2 to 3.5 cm wide and 1/5 to nearly ½ total length." (Suhm and Krieger 1954, p446)

Suhm and Krieger suggest a wide date range of 4000 BCE to 1000 CE (Suhm and Krieger 1954, p446). Anderson and Smith include it in two groups of points they date collectively to 8715-6100 BCE (Anderson and Smith, p272).

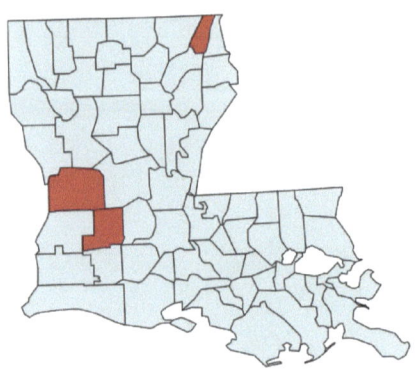
Reported Martindale Specimens

No type site is referenced by Suhm and Krieger.

<u>These points have also been identified in:</u>
Allen Parish (Digital Index of North American Archaeology 2020; Louisiana Division of Archaeology 2020)
Vernon Parish (Anderson and Smith 2003, p243; Louisiana Division of Archaeology 2020)
West Carroll Parish (Ford and Webb 1956, p63)

Maud:

"Outline: Slender triangular points with edges usually straight, sometimes recurved with constriction near middle. Bases deeply concave to deeply V-shaped. Commonly very finely chipped, thin, flat, with edges minutely serrated.

Dimensions: Length about 2 to 5.5 cm. Maximum width quite uniform at 1 to 1.5 cm. Basal concavity 0.3 to 0.7 cm." (Suhm and Krieger 1954, p504)

Suhm and Krieger estimate a date range of 1200-1500 CE, which is still the date used by Anderson and Smith today (Suhm and Krieger 1954, p504; Anderson and Smith, p295).

No type site is referenced by Suhm and Krieger.

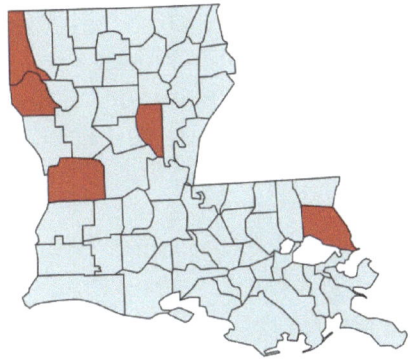

Reported Maud Specimens

These points have also been identified in:
Caddo Parish (Louisiana Division of Archaeology 2020)
DeSoto Parish (Webb 1963, p180)
LaSalle Parish (Louisiana Division of Archaeology 2020)
St. Tammany Parish (Louisiana Division of Archaeology 2020)
Vernon Parish (Anderson and Smith 2003, p243)

Maybon (also known as Mabin):
NB: This is often considered a subtype of Gary points

These points were first identified and named "Mabin" by Phillips in a 1970 publication. The first detailed description is from Williams and Brain, who consider it a subtype of the Gary point, and also change the spelling to avoid confusion with an existing pottery type:

"Lengths range from 3.6 to 5.8 cm, widths from 2 to 3 cm, and thicknesses from .5 to .8 cm. These points have the general characteristics of the [Gary] type: well-defined shoulders and contracting stems with rounded base. On the other hand, median ridges are poorly developed or absent as a result of transverse percussion flaking, so that blade faces may thus be quite flat, and the average thickness of the points is unusually thin for the type. This variety is also distinguished by the generally high degree of workmanship, and it exhibits controlled retouching of the edges, including the stem." (Williams and Brain 1983, p233)

This type is often considered a subtype of Gary points, for which the dating information would be as follows:

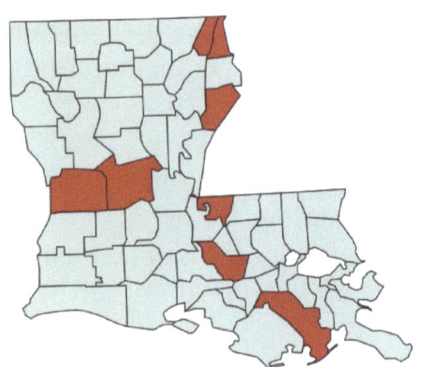

Reported Maybon Specimens

Suhm and Krieger give a date range of 2000 BCE to 1000 CE, noting a possibility of being as late as contact with Europeans (Suhm and Krieger 1954, p430). Cambron and Hulse excavated several in a late Archaic to Woodland context at the Stanfield-Worley Bluff Shelter (Cambron and Hulse 1975, p57). Justice and Kudlaty offer a slightly later date range from 1500 BCE with use continuing until 100 CE (Justice and Kudlaty 1999, p36).

No type site is referenced by Williams and Brain.

These points have also been identified in:
East Carroll Parish (Louisiana Division of Archaeology 2020)
Iberville Parish (Louisiana Division of Archaeology 2020)
Lafourche Parish (Louisiana Division of Archaeology 2020)
Rapides Parish (Digital Index of North American Archaeology 2020)
Tensas Parish (Louisiana Division of Archaeology 2020)
Vernon Parish (Digital Index of North American Archaeology 2020)
West Carroll Parish (Louisiana Division of Archaeology 2020)
West Feliciana Parish (Louisiana Division of Archaeology 2020)

Meserve:
Bell and Hall report that this description was written by E. Mott Davis and present to them for publication:

"Meserve points are like Plainview points in width, thickness, style of flaking, basal outline, and basal grinding. They are unlike Plainview points in length, general outline, and secondary treatment of tip edges and basal concavity. Many of them appear to be reworked Plainview points.

Outline: Blade edges straight, tapering, sometimes serrated; they extend back beyond midpoint and make an angle with basal edges. Blade edges sometimes inset from basal edges. Basal edges straight or slightly concave, roughly parallel. Base concave.

Secondary Treatment: Blade edges unifacially beveled, bevel being on right edge as either face is viewed with tip forward. Beveling produces rhomboidal cross-section near the tip. Unifacial beveling may or may not extend back to include basal edges. Basal edges may be retouched bifacially. Basal concavity bifacially beveled by removal of vertical flakes; sometimes one of these flakes is long, creating a short flute. Concavity and basal edges usually ground smooth." (Bell and Hall 1952, p6-7)

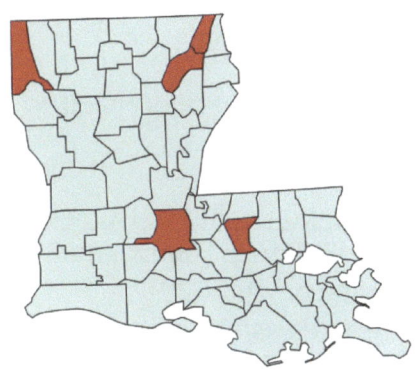

Reported Meserve Specimens

Bell suggests a date range of 7000-2000 BCE (Bell 1958, p52). Suhm and Krieger suggest that these points existed in the Paleo era, but hypothesize that most were from the Archaic, when they assert beveling was more widespread (Suhm and Krieger 1954, p450).

The type sites are the Meserve Bone Quarry Site, the Red Smoke Site, and the Gibson Site, in Hall County, Nebraska, Frontier County, Nebraska, and Taylor County, Texas, respectively (Bell 1958, p52).

These points have also been identified in:
Caddo Parish (Louisiana Division of Archaeology 2020)
East Baton Rouge Parish (Digital Index of North American Archaeology 2020; Louisiana Division of Archaeology 2020)
Richland Parish (Louisiana Division of Archaeology 2020)
St. Landry Parish (Louisiana Division of Archaeology 2020)
West Carroll Parish (Ford and Webb 1956, p63)

Morhiss:
"**Outline:** Triangular blade with edges almost always convex. Shoulders generally small, from hardly visible to right-angular. Barbs, if present, very small. Stem parallel-edged with convex base to somewhat contracted with straight to convex base. In general, stem very broad and rounded with blade not greatly wider.

Dimensions: Total length about 5 to 9 cm, average 7 to 8 cm. Maximum width across shoulders about 2.5 to 4 cm. Maximum stem width about 1.8 to 2.5 cm; stems 1/3 to 1/5 of total length." (Suhm and Krieger 1954, p454)

Suhm and Krieger give a date range of 2000 BCE to 1000 CE (Suhm and Krieger 1954, p454).

No type site is referenced by Suhm and Krieger.

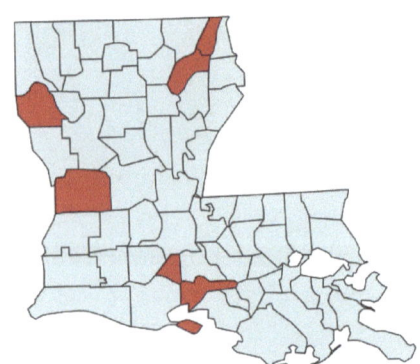
Reported Morhiss Specimens

These points have also been identified in:
DeSoto Parish (Louisiana Division of Archaeology 2020)
Iberia Parish (Gagliano 1967, p85)
Lafayette Parish (Gibson 1979, p100)
Richland Parish (Louisiana Division of Archaeology 2020)
Vernon Parish (Anderson and Smith 2003, p243; Digital Index of North American Archaeology 2020; Guderjan and Morehead 1981, p13; Louisiana Division of Archaeology 2020)
West Carroll Parish (Ford and Webb 1956, p67)

Morrill Stemmed:
"This is somewhat similar to Wells [points] but on the whole the blades are wider and longer, the stems shorter, unsmoothed, and more parallel-edges, and the bases straight. Overlaps occur with Wells points when the stems are midway between 'contracting' and 'parallel,' but the greater width and stronger shoulders that go with these stems suggest that they are Morrill rather than Wells." (Newell and Krieger 1949, p167-8)

Suhm and Krieger estimate a date range of 1000 BCE to 1000 CE (Suhm and Krieger 1954, p456).

The type site is the George C. Davis Site in Cherokee County, Texas (Newell and Krieger 1949, p167).

These points have also been identified in:
Natchitoches Parish (Digital Index of North American Archaeology 2020)
Richland Parish (Louisiana Division of Archaeology 2020)
Vernon Parish (Anderson and Smith 2003, p243; Guderjan and Morehead 1981, p13)

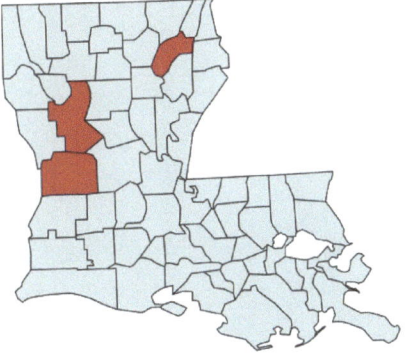

Reported Morrill Stemmed Specimens

Motley:

"**Form:** Large triangular, corner-notched, gently convex sides, well-executed blade. Notching is quite variable, but always pronounced or fairly deep; generally a rounded corner, rather than an oblique notch, is removed. Barbs are present, but never very pronounced. The stem always expands towards the base which is generally flat, though occasionally slightly convex.

Motley illustration from Cambron and Hulse 1975 (Public Domain)

Measurements:
Length: 55-98 mm; average 73 mm.
Width: 28-35 mm; average 30 mm.
Thickness: 6-12 mm; average, 8 mm.

Technique: Apparently pressure chipped, though large flakes are most frequently seen. These are always bifacial. Despite large flaking, a neat, well-executed appearance is a constant feature.

Material: Flint or chert, ranging in color from light grays through tans to jet black." (Ford et al. 1955, p129)

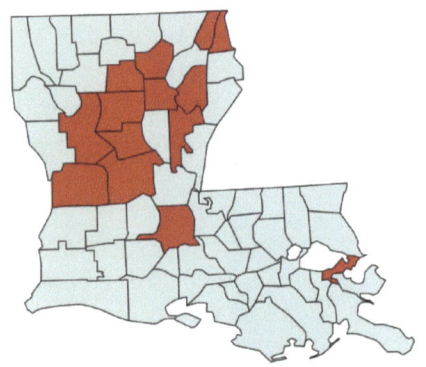

Reported Motley Specimens

Justice and Kudlaty give a date range of 1400-600 BCE (Justice and Kudlaty 1999, p34). Ford, Phillips, and Haag assigned a "probably Archaic and Poverty Point" time horizon (Ford et al. 1955, p129). Based on this point's frequent association with the Poverty Point culture, Bell gives a date range of 1300-200 BCE, based upon radiocarbon dates for various Poverty Point sites (Bell 1958, p62). Anderson and Smith give a range of 1500-500 BCE (Anderson and Smith, p275).

The type site is the Motley Place Site, adjacent to the Poverty Point Plantation Site in West Carroll Parish, Louisiana (Ford et al. 1955, p129).

These points have also been identified in:
Caldwell Parish (Louisiana Division of Archaeology 2020)
Catahoula Parish (Louisiana Division of Archaeology 2020)
East Carroll Parish (Louisiana Division of Archaeology 2020)
Franklin Parish (Griffing 1985, p239)
Grant Parish (Louisiana Division of Archaeology 2020)
Jackson Parish (Louisiana Division of Archaeology 2020)
Natchitoches Parish (Digital Index of North American Archaeology 2020)
Orleans Parish (Shenkel 1974, p57)
Ouachita Parish (Digital Index of North American Archaeology 2020)
Rapides Parish (Louisiana Division of Archaeology 2020)

St. Landry Parish (Louisiana Division of Archaeology 2020)
Vernon Parish (Anderson and Smith 2003, p243; Digital Index of North American Archaeology 2020; Louisiana Division of Archaeology 2020)
West Carroll Parish (Ford et al. 1955, p129; Ford and Webb 1956, p57; Kuttruff 1975, p135; Louisiana Division of Archaeology 2020)
Winn Parish (Digital Index of North American Archaeology 2020; Louisiana Division of Archaeology 2020)

Neches River:
Many sources cite Jelks' 1965 dissertation, but Jelks was merely using the description written by D.T. Kent, Jr, who had sent copies in letters to archaeologists sometime in the early 1960s, including Lathel Duffield. This description was never published until 2015 when it resurfaced as part of the papers of Kent and was quoted in full by Woods, supposedly from the final draft of the original letter:

"**Outline:** The Neches River point has a crudely triangular blade and an expanded stem. The blade edges are usually straight to convex, but can be slightly concave and/or recurved. The shoulders, which are generally slightly rounded, can vary to weakly barbed forms. A trait characteristic of these points is the slight to very prominent serrations beginning at the shoulders and extending upwards ½ to 2/3 the length of the blade edge. Above the serrations fine, well-spaced, secondary flaking produces a thinning of the remaining blade edge, face and tip. When this secondary flaking is concentrated on opposite faces and edges a prominent bevel is produced.

The stem, which is always expanded, is generally formed by corner notches and it varies from ¼ to 1/3 of the total length of the point. The base is straight to slightly convex. Specimens which have a convex base tend to have a bulbous stem due to the angle at which the stem edges and base meet. The base is always bifacially thinned by removal of one or more flakes, the scars of which rarely extend past the shoulders of the point. Which this thinning of the base and blade tip, the point is generally thickest at the juncture of the blade and stem.

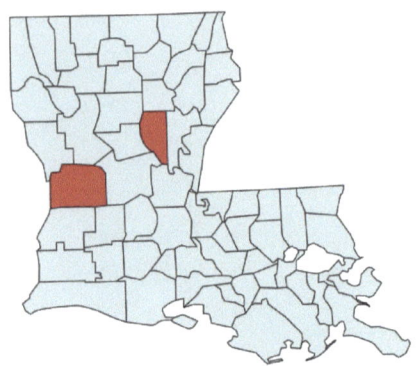

Reported Neches River Specimens

Dimensions: The Neches River point is a small to medium size dart point whose length ranges from 2.9 cm to 5.3 cm with the average specimen being 4.4 cm. In thickness the points vary from 0.5 cm to 1 cm with the average being 0.8 cm. In width at the shoulders the blade ranges from 1.6 cm to 2.8 cm with an average of 2.2 cm." (Woods 2015, p11-2)

Woods reports that Kent estimated an age range of 1000 BCE to 1000 CE (Woods 2015, p12). Anderson and Smith suggest this type is contemporaneous with the Sinner type (Anderson and Smith, p275).

No type site is referenced by Kent, as reported by Woods.

These points have also been identified in:
LaSalle Parish (Louisiana Division of Archaeology 2020)
Vernon Parish (Anderson and Smith 2003, p243)

Nodena (also known as Nodena Elliptical):
This point is first named in a 1955 publication by Chapman and Anderson, but is first fully described by Bell.

"The Nodena point is a finely chipped, willow-leaf shaped arrow point. The outline is one of a slender pointed ellipse, the base usually being rounded and not set off from the blade. In some examples the base is more pointed, rather than rounded, forming a double-pointed specimen. The points are widest in the mid-section area with the greatest width commonly falling toward the basal end of the specimen. The type is characterized by fine workmanship, the point having been made from a thin flake by careful pressure chipping.

Nodena illustration from Cambron and Hulse 1975 (Public Domain)

In size, the Nodena point ranges from about 1 to 3 inches in length, the great majority of specimens, however, fall between 1¼ and 2 inches." (Bell 1958, p64)

Justice and Kudlaty give a date range of 1400-1700 CE (Justice and Kudlaty 1999, p44). Often found in caches for burials, Bell dates these points from 1400 to 1600 CE (Bell 1958, p64). Webb agrees with the 1400-1600 CE dating (Webb 1981, p17).

The type site is the Nodena Site in Mississippi County, Arkansas (Bell 1958, p64).

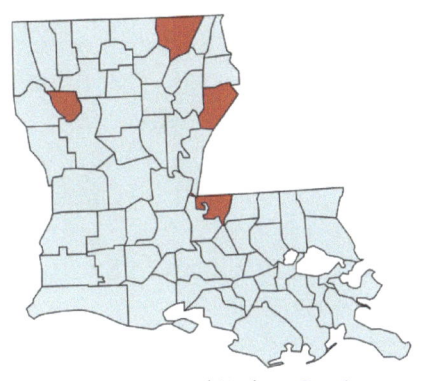

Reported Nodena Specimens

These points have also been identified in:
Morehouse Parish (Louisiana Division of Archaeology 2020)
Red River Parish (Louisiana Division of Archaeology 2020)
Tensas Parish (Digital Index of North American Archaeology 2020; Louisiana Division of Archaeology 2020)
West Feliciana Parish (Louisiana Division of Archaeology 2020)

Nolan (sometimes Nolan Beveled in older publications):
First named by Kelley in 1947 as the Nolan Beveled, the first formal description was in Suhm and Krieger's famous <u>Introductory Handbook of Texas Archaeology:</u>

"**Outline:** Triangular blade of greatly variable length and width, edges convex or recurved, seldom straight. A slender, needle-sharp tip often results from convergence of recurved edges. Shoulders may be almost absent but usually strong and slant toward tip; barbs absent. Stem varies from narrow to broad, generally parallel-edged but sometimes expanded or contracted slightly. Bases usually straight but may be convex and in rare cases slightly concave. The type is most easily recognized by strong, steep bevels on the stem, usually along the right edge of both faces, occasionally on left edge. Rarely, blade is beveled, too.

Dimensions: Total length about 4.5 to 13 cm. Maximum width 2 to 4 cm. Stems 1.1 to 3 cm wide but most between 1.5 and 2 cm. Stem length fairly uniform at about 2 cm from base to top of curve into shoulder." (Suhm and Krieger 1954, p458)

Suhm and Krieger give a date range of 4000 BCE to 1000 CE (Suhm and Krieger 1954, p458). Anderson and Smith offer a date of 4800-3100 BCE that is commonly used in Texas (Anderson and Smith, p276).

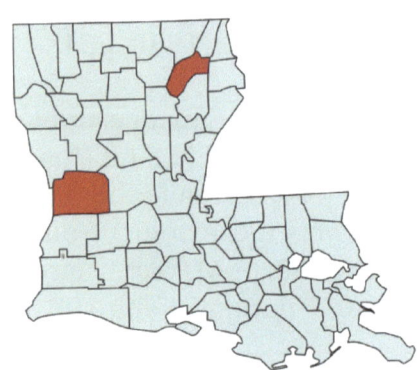

Reported Nolan Specimens

The type site is the Lehmann Rock Shelter in Gillespie County, Texas, though earlier examples were recognized by Kelley at the time of naming (Kelley 1947, p125).

<u>These points have also been identified in:</u>
Richland Parish (Louisiana Division of Archaeology 2020)
Vernon Parish (Anderson and Smith 2003, p243)

Opossum Bayou:

"...they are thick and crudely percussion flaked. They are corner or side notched, and have convex bases which may be thinned and shoulders are slightly barbed, straight, or slightly contracting. Treatment of the distal end and blade is similar to that given the Denton points, with beveled and rounded distal ends represented and with all but one specimen exhibiting some smoothing of blade edges, which are usually convex.

Measurements for the fifteen specimens from the site are:
length – range 38-70 mm, average 58.8 mm;
width – range 25-38 mm, average 32.7 mm;
thickness – range 6-13 mm, average 10.5 mm;
stem width at construction – range 16-26 mm, average 20.6 mm.

They are made of tan, yellow, gray, and brown local chert." (Connaway 1977, p28)

Connaway assigns these points a similar time range as the Denton points, which they are apparently contemporaneous with, which would be 3000 BCE and prior (Connaway 1977, p30).

The type site is the Denton Site in Quitman County, Mississippi (Connaway 1977, p28).

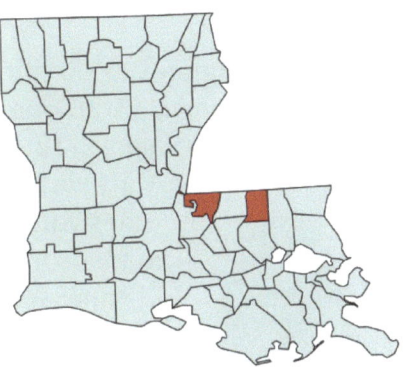

Reported Opossum Bayou Specimens

These points have also been identified in:
St. Helena Parish (Louisiana Division of Archaeology 2020)
West Feliciana Parish (Louisiana Division of Archaeology 2020)

Palmer:
"A small corner-notched blade with a straight, ground base and pronounced serrations.

Form:
(1) Blade: Small and triangular. The ratio of width to length varied from 1:1 to 1:2.5 with the average being about 1:1.5. The sides were occasionally rounded or concave, but usually straight. Most specimens were serrated, some quite deeply.
(2) Base: Straight and ground. One of the most characteristic traits of this type was the thorough grinding of the base.
(3) Corner-notches: The typical point had a small, narrow, U-shaped corner-notch that averaged about 3 mm in width and 5 to 7 mm in length when measured on the stem. These notches were precisely made in the corner of the triangular blade in such a way that the bottom of the notch formed projecting barbs. The width of these barbs usually exceeded the width of the base.

Size:
(1) Length: Range, 28-60 mm; average, 35 mm.
(2) Width: Range, 15-25 mm; average, 20 mm.
(3) Thickness: Range, 5-12 mm; average; 8mm.

Palmer Illustration from Cambron and Hulse 1975 (Public Domain)

Material: Most specimens were made from argillite, novaculite, or some other variety of the silicified slates. About ten per cent of the group was made from white vein quartz and two specimens were made from blue "Tennessee" chert which occurs locally in the Triassic gravel beds.

Technique of manufacture: These points were made by pressure flaking upon a prismatic flake of the proper proportions. The serrations, apparently, were made at the time the point was finished, since the flake scars produced by the serrations were long and overlapped toward the center of the blade. The bases were ground until they were straight." (Coe 1964, p67)

Coe assumed a date of around 7700 BCE based upon similarities to Dalton types (Coe 1964, p120). Cambron and Hulse suggest using a date of around 6,000 BCE based upon Coe's work (Cambron and Hulse 1975, p101). Ward and Davis offer a slightly earlier date of 8000-7000 BCE (p55).

The type site is the Hardaway Site in Stanly County, North Carolina (Coe 1964, p67).

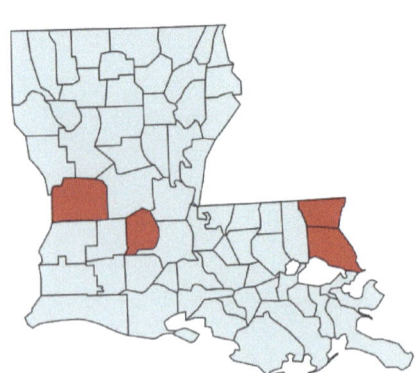

Reported Palmer Specimens

These points have also been identified in:
Evangeline Parish (Louisiana Division of Archaeology 2020)
St. Tammany Parish (Louisiana Division of Archaeology 2020)

Vernon Parish (Anderson and Smith 2003, p243; Louisiana Division of Archaeology 2020)
Washington Parish (Louisiana Division of Archaeology 2020)

Palmillas:

The original description of Palmillas points by Richard "Scotty" MacNeish is in a Spanish-language journal that was not immediately available, and the author also does not speak Spanish at a level for scholarly articles. This description is also by MacNeish in from the massive English-language publication, <u>Prehistory of the Tehuacan Valley.</u>

"Dimensions in cm:
Length: 3.8-5.7, average 4.5
Width: 2.1-4.0, average 2.9
Thickness: 0.5-1.0, average 0.6
Stem Length: 0.7-1.5, average 1.1
Stem Width: 1.1-2.6, average 1.4

These corner-notched points have expanding stems with convex bases. The long, triangular bodies have convex edges and tapering tips. The shoulder barbs point downward at about a 45-degree angle from the main axis of the projectile point.

The long triangular blanks from which these points were fashioned may have been made by percussion chipping. The surfaces and edges were reworked by a suitable pressure or percussion technique. The corner notches seem to have been made by single percussion blows struck on opposite surfaces, but the barbs and stems have been further retouched." (MacNeish et al. 1967, p72)

MacNeish roughly dates Palmillas as fairly late, extending into historic times (MacNeish et al. 1967, p72). Suhm and Krieger merely give the estimate of "probably within Christian era" (Suhm and Krieger 1954, p462). Anderson and Smith also decline to offer a specific date range, citing the ambiguous nature of the description as the source of much consternation in establishing a type narrow enough to warrant dating (Anderson and Smith, p277).

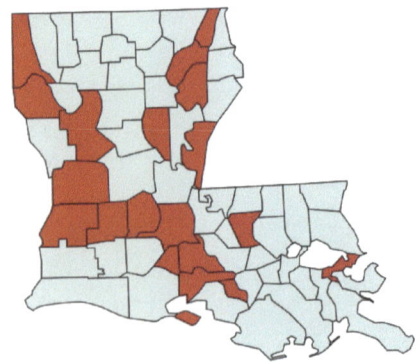

Reported Palmillas Specimens

No type site is referenced by MacNeish, but were first identified in Tamaulipas, Mexico (MacNeish et al. 1967, p72).

<u>These points have also been identified in:</u>
Allen Parish (Digital Index of North American Archaeology 2020; Louisiana Division of Archaeology 2020)
Beauregard Parish (Louisiana Division of Archaeology 2020)
Caddo Parish (Louisiana Division of Archaeology 2020)
Concordia Parish (Louisiana Division of Archaeology 2020)
DeSoto Parish (Louisiana Division of Archaeology 2020)

East Baton Rouge Parish (Gagliano 1963, p113)
Evangeline Parish (Louisiana Division of Archaeology 2020)
Franklin Parish (Digital Index of North American Archaeology 2020; Louisiana Division of Archaeology 2020)
Iberia Parish (Gagliano 1967, p85)
Lafayette Parish (Gibson 1979, p100)
LaSalle Parish (Louisiana Division of Archaeology 2020)
Natchitoches Parish (Smith 1975, p184)
Orleans Parish (Shenkel 1974, p57; Shenkel and Holley 1974, p235)
Richland Parish (Louisiana Division of Archaeology 2020)
St. Landry Parish (Louisiana Division of Archaeology 2020)
St. Martin Parish (Louisiana Division of Archaeology 2020)
Vernon Parish (Anderson and Smith 2003, p243; Digital Index of North American Archaeology 2020)
West Carroll Parish (Ford and Webb 1956, p63)

Pelican:
These were first named in a 1965 publication by Gagliano and Gregory, but formally described by Perino:

"These points, lanceolate and basally ground, seem to be local Paleo-Indian variations of the more typical point types. The Pelican point is characterized by a short stubby blade, with its greatest width over three-fourths of the way to the point. This shortness and width – the widest portion of the blade often equals the length of the projectile – gives these artifacts an awkward appearance. Workmanship is often very good and the points seem possibly to be the products of people working local material. All were made of chert which imposed some severe limitations on the type." (Perino 1968, p66)

Anderson and Smith tentatively suggest a date range of 10900-9450 BCE based on morphological similarities to other middle and late Paleoindian points (Anderson and Smith, p277).

There is no type site, but the first specimens were from Natchitoches Parish, Louisiana according to Perino (Perino 1968, p66). Webb, however, reports that the type site is on San Patricio Creek near the town of Pelican in DeSoto Parish (Webb 1981, p4).

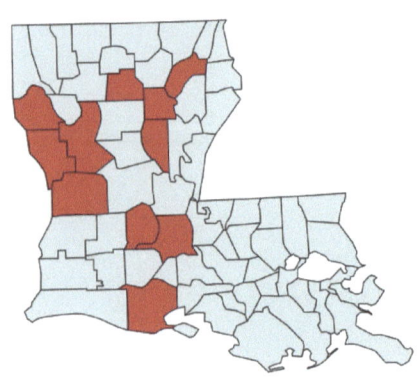
Reported Pelican Specimens

These points have also been identified in:
Beauregard Parish (Digital Index of North American Archaeology 2020)
Caldwell Parish (Digital Index of North American Archaeology 2020)
DeSoto Parish (Webb 1981, p4)
Evangeline Parish (Louisiana Division of Archaeology 2020)
Jackson Parish (Digital Index of North American Archaeology 2020)
LaSalle Parish (Digital Index of North American Archaeology 2020; Louisiana Division of Archaeology 2020)
Natchitoches Parish (Louisiana Division of Archaeology 2020; Perino 1968, p66)
Richland Parish (Digital Index of North American Archaeology 2020)
Sabine Parish (Louisiana Division of Archaeology 2020)
St. Landry Parish (Louisiana Division of Archaeology 2020)
Vermilion Parish (Digital Index of North American Archaeology 2020; Louisiana Division of Archaeology 2020)
Vernon Parish (Anderson and Smith 2003, p243; Louisiana Division of Archaeology 2020)

Perdiz (also known as Foyle Flake):
Originally named in a 1947 publication by Kelley, this point was first described in the famous Introductory Handbook of Texas Archaeology:

"**Outline:** Triangular blade with edges usually quite straight but sometimes slightly convex or concave. Shoulders sometimes at right angles to stem but usually well barbed. Stem contracted, often quite sharp at base, but may be somewhat rounded. Occasionally, specimen may be worked on one face only, or mainly on one face. More variation in size and proportions than in most arrow-point types in Texas. Workmanship generally good, sometimes exceedingly fine with minutely serrated blade edges.

Dimensions: Total length about 1.5 to 6 cm, the longer specimens overlapping several dart point types in length but much thinner and lighter than specimens classified as dart points. Maximum width about 1.2 to 3 cm. Stems 0.5 to 1.5 cm long, generally ½ to 1/7 of total length." (Suhm and Krieger 1954, p504)

Suhm and Krieger give a range of 1000-1500 CE (Suhm and Krieger 1954, p504). Webb gives a range of 1000-1300 CE (Webb 1981, p16). Anderson and Smith give a range of 1200-1500 CE, noting that the type spreads rapidly after 1200 in Texas (Anderson and Smith, p295).

No type site is referenced by Suhm and Krieger or Kelley.

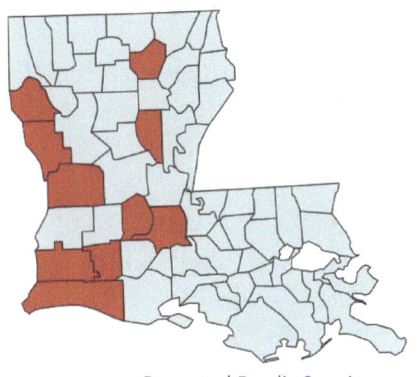
Reported Perdiz Specimens

These points have also been identified in:
Beauregard Parish (Louisiana Division of Archaeology 2020)
Calcasieu Parish (Louisiana Division of Archaeology 2020)
Cameron Parish (Louisiana Division of Archaeology 2020)
DeSoto Parish (Digital Index of North American Archaeology 2020; Louisiana Division of Archaeology 2020)
Evangeline Parish (Louisiana Division of Archaeology 2020)
Jefferson Davis Parish (Louisiana Division of Archaeology 2020)
LaSalle Parish (Louisiana Division of Archaeology 2020)
Ouachita Parish (Digital Index of North American Archaeology 2020; Louisiana Division of Archaeology 2020)
Sabine Parish (Louisiana Division of Archaeology 2020)
St. Landry Parish (Louisiana Division of Archaeology 2020)
Vernon Parish (Anderson and Smith 2003, p243; Digital Index of North American Archaeology 2020; Louisiana Division of Archaeology 2020)

Plainview:
Plainview points were first illustrated by Sellards, Evans, Meade, and Krieger in a 1947 publication, and also described by Krieger that same year:

"...has the irregular chipping which is most common in the Plainview series. The edges of most specimens are parallel but some expand very slightly at about the midpoint. None are widest beyond the midpoint in the typical Folsom Fluted fashion.

In length they vary from about 2½ to 3½ inches, longer than most Folsoms and more like Clovis Fluted. The basal concavity is shallow and compound, rounding into the basal corners exactly as in Clovis Fluted, and hence different from Folsom. Generally speaking, the Plainview points strongly suggest Clovis Fluted in most respects, except of course the absence of fluting.

The collateral chipping, on the other hand, suggests some relationship with the Eden Yuma, even though there is great difference in the shape and proportions. The basal edges of Plainview points, in all but one case, are well smoothed." (Krieger 1947b, p17-8)

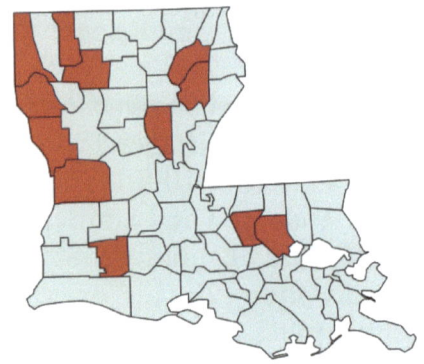

Reported Plainview Specimens

Webb suggests a date range of 7000-6000 BCE (Webb 1981, p3). Suhm and Krieger give a date range of 7000-2000 BCE (Suhm and Krieger 1954, p472). Bell notes radiocarbon dates that put the Plainview in use at least from 9670-7260 BCE (Bell 1958, p74). Boszhardt prefers a narrow range of use from 8000-7000 BCE (Boszhardt 2003, p21). Justice and Kudlaty simply give a date of 8000 BCE (Justice and Kudlaty 1999, p4).

The type site is the Plainview Site in Hale County, Texas (Krieger 1947a).

<u>These points have also been identified in:</u>
Bienville Parish (Louisiana Division of Archaeology 2020)
Caddo Parish (Louisiana Division of Archaeology 2020)
DeSoto Parish (Louisiana Division of Archaeology 2020)
East Baton Rouge Parish (Gagliano 1963, p113)
Franklin Parish (Digital Index of North American Archaeology 2020)
Jefferson Davis Parish (Louisiana Division of Archaeology 2020)
LaSalle Parish (Digital Index of North American Archaeology 2020)
Livingston Parish (Digital Index of North American Archaeology 2020)
Richland Parish (Louisiana Division of Archaeology 2020)
Sabine Parish (Louisiana Division of Archaeology 2020)
Vernon Parish (Anderson and Smith 2003, p243)
Webster Parish (Digital Index of North American Archaeology 2020)
West Carroll Parish (Ford and Webb 1956, p64)

Pontchartrain:

"These are narrow points, two to three and one half times longer than the width; about three times seems most characteristic. Typically, the blades have nearly parallel edges for most of their length, but occasionally the edges are slightly convex.

These points, relatively thick in section, usually have median ridges that give them a diamond-shaped cross-section. On 33 percent, the ridge occurs only on one face, with the opposite face rounded or flat, giving a triangular section. Thirteen percent are lenticular in section.

Very well-executed ripple flaking, with flake scars often extending from blade edge nearly to the median ridge, is a feature of typical Pontchartrain. This may occur on only one face, but usually is found on both.

The shoulders are slight but definite, barbless, and either square or slightly sloping. Stems are relatively wide and tend to be squared; a few are mildly tapering. Straight or very slightly convex or concave stem bases are usual.

The lengths range from 4.8 to 9.5 cm; 6 to 8 cm is usual. Most of these points are made of tan chert." (Ford and Webb 1956, p54-5)

NB: Ford and Webb noted that roughly 10 percent of the 231 specimens at Poverty Point were weakly corner notched, despite this not being in the description for "Pontchartrain, Typical."

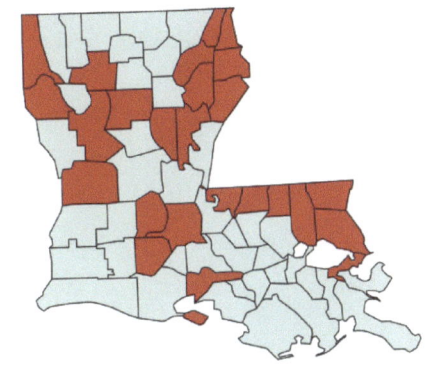

Reported Pontchartrain Specimens

Geiger dates these points to 1300-200 BCE based upon their association with Poverty Point and Tchefuncte cultural sites (Geiger 1980, p19). Ford and Webb generally put the Poverty Point site where they named this point in the late Archaic, from 1300-200 BCE, though they tentatively narrow it to 800-600 BCE (Ford and Webb 1956, p124).

The type site is Poverty Point in West Carroll Parish, Louisiana (Ford and Webb 1956, p54).

These points have also been identified in:
Acadia Parish (Louisiana Division of Archaeology 2020)
Bienville Parish (Louisiana Division of Archaeology 2020)
Caddo Parish (Louisiana Division of Archaeology 2020)
Catahoula Parish (Digital Index of North American Archaeology 2020; Gibson 1975, p203; Louisiana Division of Archaeology 2020)
DeSoto Parish (Louisiana Division of Archaeology 2020; Webb 1963, p177; Webb 1981, p9)
East Carroll Parish (Louisiana Division of Archaeology 2020)
East Feliciana Parish (Louisiana Division of Archaeology 2020)

Evangeline Parish (Louisiana Division of Archaeology 2020)
Franklin Parish (Griffing 1985, p239; Louisiana Division of Archaeology 2020)
Iberia Parish (Gagliano 1967, p85; Louisiana Division of Archaeology 2020; Neuman 1984, p84)
LaSalle Parish (Hunter 1970, p84; Louisiana Division of Archaeology 2020)
Madison Parish (Gregory et al. 1970, p42; Louisiana Division of Archaeology 2020)
Natchitoches Parish (Louisiana Division of Archaeology 2020; Smith 1975, p184)
Orleans Parish (Louisiana Division of Archaeology 2020; Shenkel 1974, p57)
Richland Parish (Louisiana Division of Archaeology 2020)
St. Helena Parish (Louisiana Division of Archaeology 2020)
St. Landry Parish (Louisiana Division of Archaeology 2020)
St. Tammany Parish (Louisiana Division of Archaeology 2020)
Tangipahoa Parish (Louisiana Division of Archaeology 2020)
Tensas Parish (Louisiana Division of Archaeology 2020)
Vernon Parish (Anderson and Smith 2003, p243; Digital Index of North American Archaeology 2020)
Washington Parish (Louisiana Division of Archaeology 2020)
West Carroll Parish (Ford and Webb 1956, p54; Kuttruff 1975, p135)
West Feliciana Parish (Louisiana Division of Archaeology 2020)
Winn Parish (Louisiana Division of Archaeology 2020)

Reed:
"...the side of the point below the notch shows a change in direction, either being straight (parallel-sided) or contracting – the side notches of this type are set close to the base so that the extent of the side below the notch is generally not more than 3 mm. In addition, the area below the notch is generally rounded rather than straight-sided. The basal area is either straight, concave, or slightly convex, this variation being regarded as an alternative feature. Slight serrations may appear on the body but are not common." (Baerreis 1954, p44)

Webb gives a date range of 1000-1100 CE (Webb 1981, p17). Bell proposes an estimated range of 500-1500 CE (Bell 1958, p76).

The type site is the Reed Site and Huffaker Sites in Delaware County, Oklahoma (Webb 1981, p17).

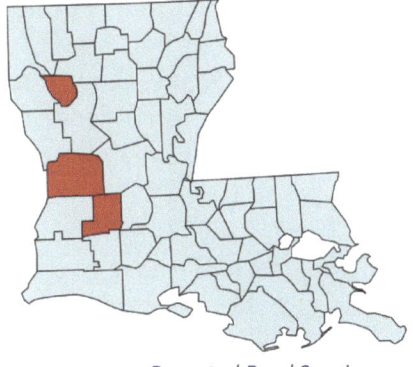

Reported Reed Specimens

These points have also been identified in:
Allen Parish (Louisiana Division of Archaeology 2020)
Red River Parish (Webb 1981, p17)
Vernon Parish (Anderson and Smith 2003, p243)

San Patrice:

"These points are of medium size, between the small arrow points (commonly termed 'bird points') and the large projectiles which are thought to be atlatl lance points. They range from 2.5 to 5 cm in length, 2 to 3.2 cm in width, and are typically thin, 4 to 7 mm at the thickest section. They are made from various materials... these points are well made, symmetrical, with carefully executed chipping and flaking.

The typical artifact is unhafted, with concave base, the concavity usually being deep and occasionally V-shaped. The edges are always concave in the basal portion, usually straight or convex in the upper portion, producing a well-defined shoulder at the level of greatest width. If the upper or blade segment of the edge is convex, the points are rather obtuse; if straight or concave, the points are acute. The length of the concave basal segment of the edge varies, the shoulder in the typical specimen being near the middle. In other instances the basal segment is longer or shorter. If very short, this concave portion produces a distinct notch.

Characteristic of these projectile points, in addition to the concavity of the base, is a thinning of the basal segment by a wide groove on each face, effected by the removal of one to three longitudinal flakes. This grooving extends from the basal concavity to or beyond the level of the shoulder, involving one-third to two-thirds of the total length of each face. In some instances there is a short groove on one face and a much longer groove on the reverse. This grooving produces an inverted Y-shaped ridge on each face, the ridge seldom being very high because of the thinness of the artifacts.

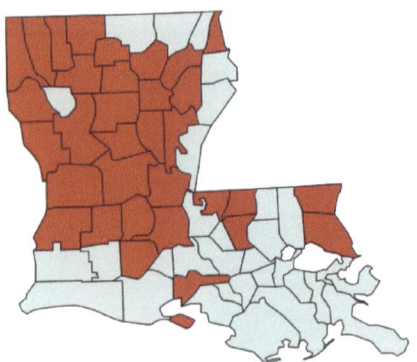

Reported San Patrice Specimens

The basal portion of each edge is moderately smooth, while the upper portion is brought to a good blade by secondary flaking in most instances. Unless the artifact is quite wide, the primary flaking of the faces extends from the edge to the inverted Y ridge." (Webb 1946, p14-5)

Geiger recommends a date of circa 8000 BCE (Geiger 1980, p17). Bell prefers a date range of 3000 BCE to 0 CE (Bell 1958, p84). Suhm and Krieger are more conservative and simply suggest an Archaic date (Suhm and Krieger 1954, p477). Webb himself later suggested a date range of 7000-6000 BCE (Webb 1981, p3). Anderson and Smith give a range of 10900-8200 BCE based upon an assumption of contemporaneity with Dalton types (Anderson and Smith, p282).

The type site is on San Patricio Creek in DeSoto Parish, Louisiana (Webb 1946, p14; Webb 1981, p3).

These points have also been identified in:

Acadia Parish (Louisiana Division of Archaeology 2020)
Allen Parish (Louisiana Division of Archaeology 2020)
Avoyelles Parish (Louisiana Division of Archaeology 2020)
Beauregard Parish (Louisiana Division of Archaeology 2020)
Bienville Parish (Louisiana Division of Archaeology 2020; Webb 1981, p3)
Bossier Parish (Louisiana Division of Archaeology 2020; Webb 1981, p3)
Caddo Parish (Digital Index of North American Archaeology 2020; Louisiana Division of Archaeology 2020; Neuman 1984, p71; Webb 1946, p14; Webb 1981, p3)
Caldwell Parish (Louisiana Division of Archaeology 2020)
Catahoula Parish (Digital Index of North American Archaeology 2020)
Claiborne Parish (Louisiana Division of Archaeology 2020)
DeSoto Parish (Digital Index of North American Archaeology 2020; Louisiana Division of Archaeology 2020; Webb 1946, p14; Webb 1981, p3)
East Baton Rouge Parish (Digital Index of North American Archaeology 2020; Gagliano 1963, p113; Louisiana Division of Archaeology 2020)
East Carroll Parish (Louisiana Division of Archaeology 2020)
East Feliciana Parish (Digital Index of North American Archaeology 2020; Louisiana Division of Archaeology 2020)
Evangeline Parish (Louisiana Division of Archaeology 2020)
Franklin Parish (Digital Index of North American Archaeology 2020; Louisiana Division of Archaeology 2020)
Grant Parish (Digital Index of North American Archaeology 2020; Louisiana Division of Archaeology 2020)
Iberia Parish (Gagliano 1967, p85)
Jackson Parish (Digital Index of North American Archaeology 2020; Louisiana Division of Archaeology 2020)
LaSalle Parish (Digital Index of North American Archaeology 2020)
Lincoln Parish (Louisiana Division of Archaeology 2020)
Natchitoches Parish (Digital Index of North American Archaeology 2020; Louisiana Division of Archaeology 2020; Smith 1975, p184; Webb 1981, p3)
Ouachita Parish (Digital Index of North American Archaeology 2020; Louisiana Division of Archaeology 2020)
Rapides Parish (Louisiana Division of Archaeology 2020)
Richland Parish (Digital Index of North American Archaeology 2020; Louisiana Division of Archaeology 2020; Penvy 2014, p4)
Sabine Parish (Digital Index of North American Archaeology 2020; Louisiana Division of Archaeology 2020)
St. Landry Parish (Louisiana Division of Archaeology 2020)
St. Tammany Parish (Louisiana Division of Archaeology 2020)
Vernon Parish (Anderson and Smith 2003, p243; Digital Index of North American Archaeology 2020; Louisiana Division of Archaeology 2020; Guderjan and Morehead 1981, p10)
Washington Parish (Louisiana Division of Archaeology 2020)
Webster Parish (Digital Index of North American Archaeology 2020)
West Feliciana Parish (Louisiana Division of Archaeology 2020)
Winn Parish (Louisiana Division of Archaeology 2020)

Scallorn Stemmed:

This point was first named in Kelley's 1947 publication, but first described by Suhm and Krieger in the famous <u>Introductory Handbook of Texas Archaeology</u>:

"**Outline:** Broad to slender triangular blades with edges straight to convex, occasionally concave. Shoulders may be squared but usually well barbed. Stem formed by notching into corners at various angles, making it expand from a broad wedge shape to rounded extremities as wide as the shoulders. Base straight, concave, or convex... Blade edges often finely serrated.

Dimensions: Total length about 2.5 to 4.5 cm, rarely longer or shorter. Maximum width at shoulders or base fairly uniform at 1.5 to 2 cm. Stems 1/3 to 1/7 of total length." (Suhm and Krieger 1954, p506)

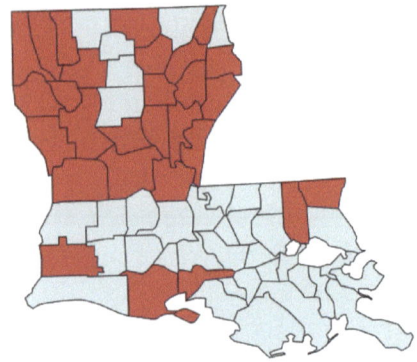

Reported Scallorn Stemmed Specimens

Suhm and Krieger give a date range of 700-1500 CE (Suhm and Krieger 1954, p506). Bell comments only that it is usually associated with late sites with both pottery and agriculture (Bell 1960, p84). Justice and Kudlaty prefer a date range of 700-1150 CE (Justice and Kudlaty 1999, p44). Webb provides a range of 500-1200 CE (Webb 1981, p16). Anderson and Smith also provide a similar range of 700-1200 CE (Anderson and Smith, p295).

The type site is the Lehmann Rock Shelter in Gillespie County, Texas (Kelley 1947, p122).

<u>These points have also been identified in:</u>
Avoyelles Parish (Louisiana Division of Archaeology 2020)
Bienville Parish (Louisiana Division of Archaeology 2020)
Bossier Parish (Digital Index of North American Archaeology 2020; Louisiana Division of Archaeology 2020)
Caddo Parish (Digital Index of North American Archaeology 2020; Louisiana Division of Archaeology 2020; Webb and McKinney 1975, p95)
Calcasieu Parish (Louisiana Division of Archaeology 2020)
Caldwell Parish (Louisiana Division of Archaeology 2020)
Catahoula Parish (Louisiana Division of Archaeology 2020)
Concordia Parish (Louisiana Division of Archaeology 2020)
DeSoto Parish (Louisiana Division of Archaeology 2020)
Franklin Parish (Griffing 1985, p239)
Grant Parish (Digital Index of North American Archaeology 2020)
Iberia Parish (Gagliano 1967, p85)
LaSalle Parish (Louisiana Division of Archaeology 2020)
Madison Parish (Louisiana Division of Archaeology 2020)

Natchitoches Parish (Louisiana Division of Archaeology 2020)
Ouachita Parish (Digital Index of North American Archaeology 2020; Louisiana Division of Archaeology 2020)
Rapides Parish (Louisiana Division of Archaeology 2020)
Red River Parish (Wright 1980, p219)
Richland Parish (Louisiana Division of Archaeology 2020)
Sabine Parish (Louisiana Division of Archaeology 2020)
Tangipahoa Parish (Digital Index of North American Archaeology 2020)
Tensas Parish (Digital Index of North American Archaeology 2020; Louisiana Division of Archaeology 2020)
Union Parish (Digital Index of North American Archaeology 2020)
Vermilion Parish (Louisiana Division of Archaeology 2020)
Vernon Parish (Anderson and Smith 2003, p243; Louisiana Division of Archaeology 2020)
Washington Parish (Louisiana Division of Archaeology 2020)
Webster Parish (Louisiana Division of Archaeology 2020)
West Carroll Parish (Ford and Webb 1956, p69)

Scottsbluff:
These points were first published by Barbour and Shultz in a 1932 publication, but the first description comes from Wormington:

"Points with somewhat triangular or parallel-sided blades, small shoulders and broad stems. The flaking is usually of the transverse parallel type, but it may be more irregular. The cross-section is a thick oval. The stem edges are usually ground. The range in length is from two to five inches. Most specimens are between three and four inches long and about one inch wide. Many of those that are less than three inches long compare with the longer specimens in breadth and may represent points that were reworked after the tips had been broken." (Wormington 1957, p267)

Bell suggests 7500-5000 BCE based upon radiocarbon dates in Nebraska and Wyoming associated with Scottsbluff points (Bell 1958, p86). Boszhardt gives a narrower range of 7200-6800 BCE (Boszhardt 2003, p29). Justice and Kudlaty provide a date range of 6800-6400 BCE (Justice and Kudlaty 1999, p6). Webb gives a date range of 7500-5000 BCE (Webb 1981, p7). Boszhardt gives a range of 7200-6800 BCE specifically for the northern plains (Boszhardt 2003, p29).

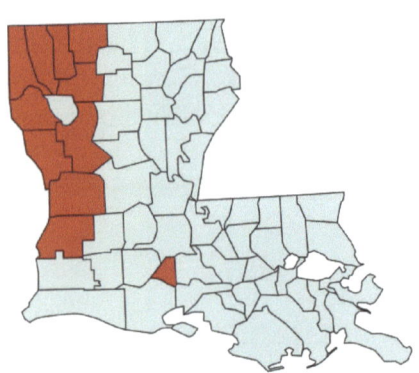
Reported Scottsbluff Specimens

The type site is the Scottsbluff Bison Quarry in Scotts Bluff County, Nebraska (Bell 1958, p86; Webb 1981, p6).

These points have also been identified in:
Beauregard Parish (Louisiana Division of Archaeology 2020)
Bienville Parish (Louisiana Division of Archaeology 2020; Webb 1981, p6)
Bossier Parish (Webb 1981, p6)
Caddo Parish (Louisiana Division of Archaeology 2020; Webb 1981, p6)
Claiborne Parish (Louisiana Division of Archaeology 2020)
DeSoto Parish (Webb 1981, p6)
Lafayette Parish (Louisiana Division of Archaeology 2020)
Natchitoches Parish (Louisiana Division of Archaeology 2020; Webb 1981, p6)
Sabine Parish (Webb 1981, p6)
Vernon Parish (Anderson and Smith 2003, p243)
Webster Parish (Webb 1981, p6)

Shumla:
These points were first published in photographs by Taylor in 1948, with the first description from Suhm and Krieger in their famous <u>Introductory Handbook of Texas Archaeology</u>:

"**Outline:** Small triangular blade with edges sometimes convex but usually straight, concave, or recurved. Almost always barbed, from short to long, sweeping out laterally, or extending into line with stem base. Stem edges more or less parallel, may expand or contract somewhat. Base usually convex, but may be straight or rarely concave. Blade edges frequently serrated.

Dimensions: Total length ranges from about 3 to 9 cm but most fall between 4 and 6 cm. Maximum width about 2.5 to 5 cm but most fall between 3 and 4 cm. Stems fairly uniform at 1 to 1.5 cm wide and 1 to 1.5 cm long; about 1/3 to 1/6 of total length." (Suhm and Krieger 1954, p480)

Suhm and Krieger put a date range of before 0 CE to 800 CE (Suhm and Krieger 1954, p480). Anderson and Smith report a range of 1200 BCE to 1775 CE based on estimates from Texas (Anderson and Smith, p283).

The type site is the Shumla Cave in Acuna Municipality, Coahuila, Mexico (Taylor 1948, p75).

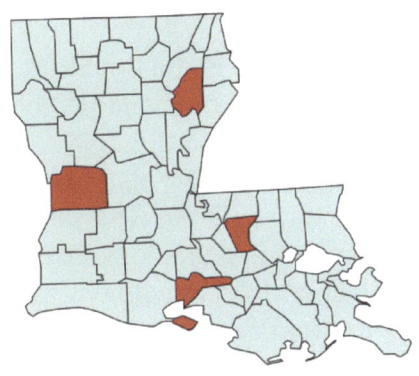
Reported Shumla Specimens

<u>These points have also been identified in:</u>
East Baton Rouge Parish (Gagliano 1963, p113)
Iberia Parish (Gagliano 1967, p85)
Franklin Parish (Griffing 1985, p239)
Vernon Parish (Anderson and Smith 2003, p243; Louisiana Division of Archaeology 2020)

Sinner:
Webb claims that this point was first named in a Webb and Gregory publication of undisclosed date, and does not provide a citation (Webb 1981, p10). The earliest description appears to come from Webb et al.:

"The Sinner type has multiple deep notches in the lower blade edges, numbering 2 to 5, and often varying in number on the two edges of a single point. Bases are squared to slightly expanded. The point is generally slender and often rough." (Webb et al. 1969, p53)

Webb states that this type is contemporaneous with the Evans type (Webb 1981, p10). Anderson and Smith use a middle Archaic range of 6876-6600 BCE based on work done at Fort Polk (Anderson and Smith, p284).

The type site is the Jim Sinner Site near Lake Bistineau in Louisiana (Webb 1981, p10).

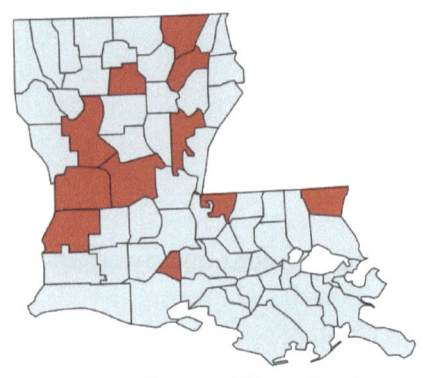

Reported Sinner Specimens

These points have also been identified in:
Beauregard Parish (Digital Index of North American Archaeology 2020; Louisiana Division of Archaeology 2020)
Catahoula Parish (Louisiana Division of Archaeology 2020)
Jackson Parish (Louisiana Division of Archaeology 2020)
Lafayette Parish (Gibson 1979, p100)
Morehouse Parish (Digital Index of North American Archaeology 2020; Louisiana Division of Archaeology 2020)
Natchitoches Parish (Louisiana Division of Archaeology 2020)
Rapides Parish (Louisiana Division of Archaeology 2020)
Richland Parish (Louisiana Division of Archaeology 2020)
Vernon Parish (Anderson and Smith 2003, p243; Digital Index of North American Archaeology 2020)
Washington Parish (Louisiana Division of Archaeology 2020)
West Feliciana Parish (Louisiana Division of Archaeology 2020)

St. Tammany:
"This projectile point with straight sides, coarse serrations, apiculate distal end, and square stems... Blades may be narrow to relatively broad. Stems are usually straight and square, but may have slightly excurvate bases. Stem edges are ground on some specimens.

Initial flakes are broad, shallow, and random. Superimposed on these along the blade edge is a series of well-executed short, deep flakes which form the serrations. These tend to be symmetrically paired, and on well-made specimens have a collateral appearance. Each of the secondary flakes had its origin on the blade margin and may extend to the median ridge. Serrations are characteristically absent from the distal ends of the points.

In cross sections, most are biconvex, but they may have prominent median ridges. A few of the longer specimens show a pronounced twist to the blade, and an occasional point is asymmetrical.

Dimensions:
Length: 44 to 85 mm; average 61 mm
Shoulder Width: 25 to 35 mm; average 28 mm
Stem Width: 17 to 26 mm; average 22 mm
Stem Length: 9 to 12 mm; average 11 mm
Thickness: 8 to 14 mm; average 11 mm" (Gagliano 1967, p4)

Gagliano dated this type to contemporaneous with Kirk types, which at the time he considered the St. Tammany point to be closely related to (Gagliano 1967, p7-8). Green suggests that this association is mistaken, and that St. Tammany are middle or late Archaic, with a range of 4550-3050 BCE (Green 2020).

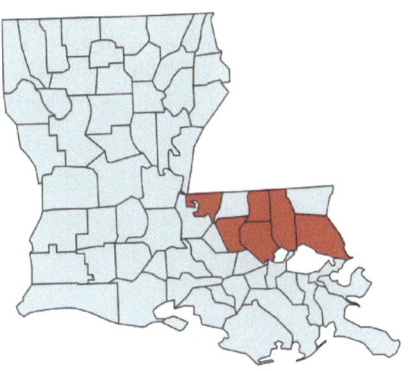
Reported St. Tammany Specimens

No type site is referenced by Gagliano, but some of the original examples were identified from St. Tammany Parish, Louisiana (Gagliano 1967, p4).

These points have also been identified in:
East Baton Rouge Parish (Gagliano 1967, p6)
Livingston Parish (Gagliano 1967, p6)
St. Helena Parish (Gagliano 1967, p5)
St. Tammany Parish (Gagliano 1967, p4)
Tangipahoa Parish (Gagliano 1967, p6)
West Feliciana Parish (Gagliano 1967, p6)

Trinity (also known as Trinity Stemmed or Trinity Notched):
This type was first illustrated and named the Trinity Stemmed by Stephenson in a 1949 illustration, and illustrated and renamed Trinity Notched by Crook and Harris in 1952, and finally described formally in the famous <u>Introductory Handbook of Texas Archaeology</u>:

"**Outline:** Blade triangular with edges straight to convex. Shoulders poorly developed due to stem being formed by two long shallow notches, crudely chipped. Stem broad, bulging laterally so as to align with blade edges, or nearly so. Base straight to strongly convex. Stem edges sometimes smoothed, base occasionally so.

Dimensions: Total length about 3 to 6 cm, average 4 to 5 cm. Maximum width across shoulders or stem, ranging from 2 to 2.5 cm. Stem ¼ to 1/3 total length, occasionally nearly ½." (Suhm and Krieger 1954, p484-6)

Suhm and Krieger give a date range of 2000-1000 BCE (Suhm and Krieger 1954, p486).

No type site is referenced, but the first example was found on the Trinity in Collin County, Texas (Stephenson 1949, p55-6).

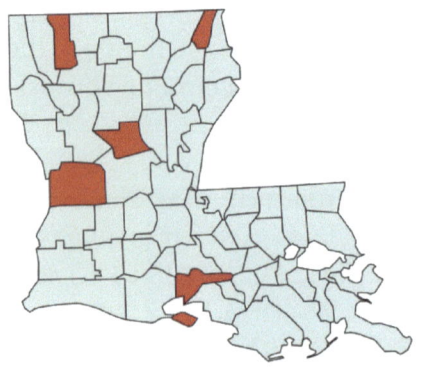

Reported Trinity Specimens

<u>These points have also been identified in:</u>
Iberia Parish (Gagliano 1967, p85)
Grant Parish (Louisiana Division of Archaeology 2020)
Webster Parish (Louisiana Division of Archaeology 2020)
West Carroll Parish (Ford and Webb 1956, p61)
Vernon Parish (Anderson and Smith 2003, p243)

Webb:

"...the blades of Webb points are broad and 'spade-shaped,' with markedly convex sides. The exceptions are more elongated, so that the edges of the blades are gently convex. Shoulders tend to be squared, slightly sloping, or barely inclined at the opposite angle so that small barbs are formed on the blade corners. Stems tend to be parallel-sided, but several have slightly contracting stems. Stem bases are straight or mildly rounded...

Large irregular flakes that occasionally extend almost entirely across the blade faces were removed in the course of the primary flaking. Blade edges are irregularly retouched. Blades are lenticular shaped in cross-section; median ridges are lacking.

Lengths range from 6.5 to 11.5 cm, averages, about 8 cm; width from 4 to 7 cm, average, about 5 cm; and thickness from 8 to 13 mm, average, 10 mm. Stem length varies from 11 to 20 mm, width from 15 to 25." (Ford and Webb 1956, p66)

Ford and Webb generally put the Poverty Point site where they named this point in the late Archaic, from 1300-200 BCE, though they tentatively narrow it to 800-600 BCE (Ford and Webb 1956, p124).

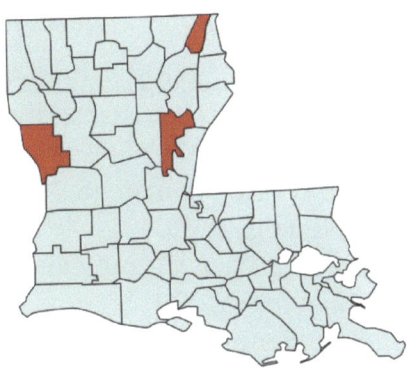

Reported Webb Specimens

The type site is Poverty Point in West Carroll Parish, Louisiana (Ford and Webb 1956, p66)

These points have also been identified in:
Catahoula Parish (Louisiana Division of Archaeology 2020)
Sabine Parish (Louisiana Division of Archaeology 2020)
West Carroll Parish (Ford and Webb 1956, p66)

Wells:
"The group is principally distinguished by very long stems which attain up to half the total length, the converging of these stems to a point or somewhat rounded base, grinding or smoothing of the stem edges on most specimens, very slight shoulders (sometimes missing on one side), and straight blade edges, sometimes serrated." (Newell et al. 1949, p167)

Suhm and Krieger estimate a date range of 1000 BCE to 1000 CE (Suhm and Krieger 1954, p488).

The type site is the George C. Davis Site in Cherokee County, Texas (Newell et al. 1949, p167).

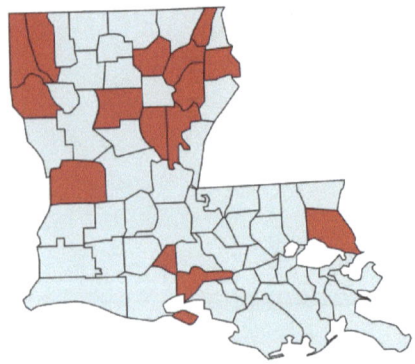

Reported Wells Specimens

These points have also been identified in:
Bossier Parish (Louisiana Division of Archaeology 2020)
Caddo Parish (Louisiana Division of Archaeology 2020)
Catahoula Parish (Louisiana Division of Archaeology 2020)
DeSoto Parish (Louisiana Division of Archaeology 2020)
Franklin Parish (Digital Index of North American Archaeology 2020)
Iberia Parish (Gagliano 1967, p85)
Lafayette Parish (Gibson 1979, p100)
LaSalle Parish (Hunter 1970, p84)
Madison Parish (Gregory et al. 1970, p42)
Ouachita Parish (Digital Index of North American Archaeology 2020)
Richland Parish (Louisiana Division of Archaeology 2020)
St. Tammany Parish (Louisiana Division of Archaeology 2020)
Vernon Parish (Anderson and Smith 2003, p243)
West Carroll Parish (Ford and Webb 1956, p64)
Winn Parish (Louisiana Division of Archaeology 2020)

Williams:

"**Outline:** Broad triangular to leaf-shaped blade with edges usually slightly to strongly convex, occasionally nearly straight. Tips sometimes slimmed to needle sharpness. Shoulders pronounced, usually well barbed. Stem formed by corner notches, always expanded, with convex base. The stem edges and base may meet at an angle, but usually stem and base form a rounded bulb.

Dimensions: Total length about 5 to 8 cm. Maximum width 2.5 to 5 cm, most between 3 and 4 cm. Stems usually between 2 and 2.5 cm wide and ¼ to 1/6 of total length." (Suhm and Krieger 1954, p490)

Suhm and Krieger suggest a date range of 4000 BCE to 1000 CE (Suhm and Krieger 1954, p490). Webb suggests the same (Webb 1981, p12). Anderson and Smith, using data from a site on Ford Polk, suggest 1770 BCE to 634 CE (Anderson and Smith 2003, p287).

No type site is referenced by Suhm and Krieger.

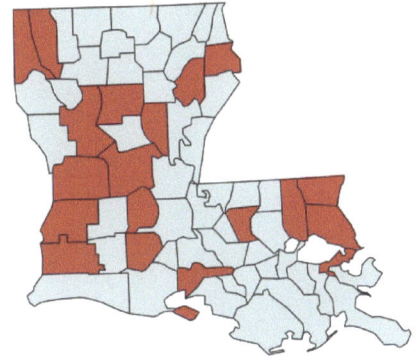

Reported Williams Specimens

These points have also been identified in:
Acadia Parish (Louisiana Division of Archaeology 2020)
Beauregard Parish (Louisiana Division of Archaeology 2020)
Bossier Parish (Louisiana Division of Archaeology 2020)
Caddo Parish (Neuman 1984, p84)
Calcasieu Parish (Louisiana Division of Archaeology 2020)
East Baton Rouge Parish (Gagliano 1963, p113)
Evangeline Parish (Louisiana Division of Archaeology 2020)
Franklin Parish (Louisiana Division of Archaeology 2020)
Iberia Parish (Gagliano 1967, p85; Louisiana Division of Archaeology 2020; Neuman 1984, p84)
LaSalle Parish (Louisiana Division of Archaeology 2020)
Madison Parish (Louisiana Division of Archaeology 2020)
Natchitoches Parish (Neuman 1984, p84; Smith 1975, p184)
Orleans Parish (Louisiana Division of Archaeology 2020)
Rapides Parish (Digital Index of North American Archaeology 2020; Louisiana Division of Archaeology 2020; Neuman 1984, p84)
Red River Parish (Louisiana Division of Archaeology 2020)
St. Tammany Parish (Digital Index of North American Archaeology 2020; Louisiana Division of Archaeology 2020)
Tangipahoa Parish (Digital Index of North American Archaeology 2020; Louisiana Division of Archaeology 2020)
Vernon Parish (Anderson and Smith 2003, p243; Digital Index of North American Archaeology 2020; Guderjan and Morehead 1981, p12; Louisiana Division of Archaeology

2020)
Washington Parish (Louisiana Division of Archaeology 2020)
Winn Parish (Digital Index of North American Archaeology 2020; Louisiana Division of Archaeology 2020)

Woden:
This type was first named and defined by Jelks in his 1965 PhD dissertation on the McGee Bend Reservoir. No copy could be located, and this description comes from Jelks' publishing of that data in 2017:

"Its most distinctive characteristic is a flat, unworked base.

Dimensions: Length, 2.5 to 8.3 cm; width, 1.5 to 3.9 cm; thickness, 0.3 to 1.2 cm.

Blade: Length, with straight, convex, or (very rarely) recurved edges; sometimes asymmetrical. Shoulders may be rounded or squared, and occasionally there are pointed shoulders that project laterally. But there are no truly barbed shoulders (that is, shoulders with sharp points projecting downward toward the base).

Stem: Approximately rectangular, moderately contracting, or (occasionally) weakly expanding. The most conspicuous attribute of the stem – and the most diagnostic criterion for identifying the type – is the flat, often thick, unworked base. In most cases, the bases are flat striking platforms where cores were struck in producing the flakes from which the points were fashioned. Prepared striking platforms evidently were seldom if ever used, so that a base usually consists of a patch of nodular cortex from the weathered surface of the chert pebble or piece of petrified wood that served as a core. Stem dimensions are: length, 0.8 to 1.8 cm; maximum width, 1.0 to 2.2 cm; maximum thickness (ordinarily at the base), 3 to 9 mm." (Jelks 2017, p143)

Anderson and Smith state that some use an early Archaic date to this point (Anderson and Smith 2003, p288), but the date is generally unsettled.

The type sites were part of the McGee Bend excavations in San Augustine, Sabine, and Nacogdoches Counties, Texas (Jelks 2017, p24).

Reported Woden Specimens

These points have also been identified in:
Vernon Parish (Anderson and Smith 2003, p243; Guderjan and Morehead 1981, p13)

Yarbrough:

This point was first named by Newell and Krieger in a difficult-to-locate 1949 article in American Antiquity, but the first widely published formal description is by Miller and Jelks:

"...a relatively slender, medium-sized dart point, with slight shoulders and a parallel-sided stem. Bases range from concave to convex and the stems are frequently smoothed along the edges." (Miller and Jelks 1952, p172)

A more complete description comes from Suhm and Krieger a couple years later:

"**Outline:** Small, slender triangular blade with edges straight to slightly convex, sometimes asymmetrical. Shoulders from small to prominent, not barbed. Stem edges parallel to somewhat expanded and often ground smooth. Base usually straight but may be slightly concave or convex. Blade sometimes beveled, usually along right edge of both faces.

Dimensions: Total length about 3.5 to 8 cm, most between 5 and 6 cm. Maximum width 1.6 to 2.5 cm, most about 2 cm. Stem width 1 to 1.5 cm and stem length consistently about 1/3 to ¼ of total length." (Suhm and Krieger 1954, p492)

Suhm and Krieger put a date range of 500 BCE to 1000 CE on Yarborough points (Suhm and Krieger 1954, p492). Miller and Jelks mainly note that this type is mainly associated with late preceramic Archaic in East Texas, with a few holdover examples found associated with pottery (Miller and Jelks 1952, p172-5). Using Fort Polk data, Anderson and Smith give a range of 4600-2500 BCE (Anderson and Smith 2003, p288).

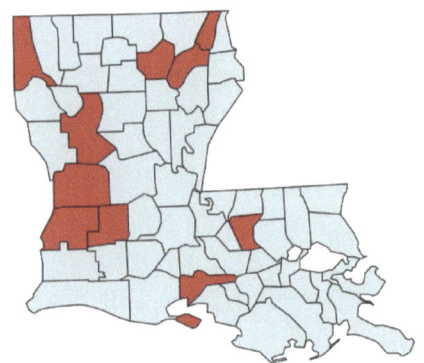

Reported Yarbrough Specimens

The type site is the Yarborough Site in Van Zandt County, Texas (Miller and Jelks 1952, p172).

These points have also been identified in:
Allen Parish (Louisiana Division of Archaeology 2020)
Beauregard Parish (Louisiana Division of Archaeology 2020)
Bossier Parish (Louisiana Division of Archaeology 2020)
Caddo Parish (Louisiana Division of Archaeology 2020)
East Baton Rouge Parish (Louisiana Division of Archaeology 2020)
Iberia Parish (Gagliano 1967, p85)
Natchitoches Parish (Louisiana Division of Archaeology 2020)
Ouachita Parish (Louisiana Division of Archaeology 2020)
Richland Parish (Louisiana Division of Archaeology 2020)
Vernon Parish (Anderson and Smith 2003, p243; Digital Index of North American

Archaeology 2020; Guderjan and Morehead 1981, p10; Louisiana Division of Archaeology 2020)
West Carroll Parish (Ford and Webb 1956, p61)

Works Cited

Anderson, David G. and Steven D. Smith. 2003. <u>Archaeology, History, and Predictive Modeling: Research at Ford Polk, 1972-2002.</u> University of Alabama Press. Tuscaloosa, Alabama.

Baerreis, David A. 1954. "The Huffaker Site, Delaware County, Oklahoma." *Bulletin of the Oklahoma Anthropological Society, Vol. 2.* p35-48.

Baker, William S. and Clarence H. Webb. 1977. "Catahoula Type Projectile Points." *Louisiana Archaeology, No. 3.* p225-251.

Bell, Robert E. 1958. <u>Guide to the Identification of Certain American Indian Projectile Points.</u> *Special Bulletin No. 1.* Oklahoma Anthropological Society.

Bell, Robert E. 1960. <u>Guide to the Identification of Certain American Indian Projectile Points.</u> *Special Bulletin No. 2.* Oklahoma Anthropological Society.

Boszhardt, Robert F. 2003. <u>A Projectile Point Guide for The Upper Mississippi River Valley.</u> University of Iowa Press. Iowa City, Iowa.

Broyles, Bettye J. 1966. "Preliminary Report: The St. Albans Site (46Ka27), Kanawha County, West Virginia." *The West Virginia Archeologist No. 19.* West Virginia Archeological Society. Moundsville, West Virginia.

Cambron, James W., and David C. Hulse. 1975. <u>Handbook of Alabama Archaeology.</u> The Archaeological Research Association of Alabama, Inc.

Carpenter, Steve and Pierre Paquin. 2010. "Towards a Genealogy of Texas Stone Projectile Points." *Bulletin of the Texas Archeological Society Vol. 81.* Lubbock, Texas. p153-176.

Chapman, Carl H. 1948. "A Preliminary Survey of Missouri Archaeology: Part IV." *The Missouri Archaeologist, Vol. 10, Part 4.*

Coe, Joffre Lanning. 1964. <u>The Formative Cultures of the Carolina Piedmont.</u> Transactions of the American Philosophical Society 54, Part 5. American Philosophical Society. Philadelphia, Pennsylvania.

Connaway, John M. 1977. <u>The Denton Site: A Middle Archaic Occupation in the Northern Yazoo Basin, Mississippi.</u> *Archaeological Report No. 4.* Mississippi Department of Archives and History. Jackson, Mississippi.

Crook, Jr. Wilson W. and R.K. Harris. 1952. "Trinity Aspect of the Archaic Horizon: The Carrollton and Elam Foci." *Bulletin of the Texas Archeological Society Vol. 23.* p7-38.

Digital Index of North American Archaeology. Louisiana Archaeological Site File Database. Search query June 2020.

Ford, James A., Philip Phillips, and William G. Haag. 1955. <u>The Jakestown Site in West Central Mississippi.</u> *American Museum of Natural History Anthropological Papers, Vol. 45, Part 1.* The American Museum of Natural History. New York, New York.

Ford, James A. and Clarence H. Webb. 1956. <u>Poverty Point, a Late Archaic Site in Louisiana.</u> *Anthropological Papers of the American Museum of Natural History, Vol. 46, Part 1.* New York, New York.

Gagliano, Sherwood M. 1963. "A Survey of Preceramic Occupations in Portions of South Louisiana and South Mississippi." *Florida Anthropologist, Vol. 16, No. 4.* p105-32.

Gagliano, Sherwood M. 1967. "Kirk Serrated: An Early Archaic Index Point in Louisiana." *Florida Anthropologist, Vol. 20, No. 1-2.* p3-9.

Gagliano, Sherwood M. 1967. <u>Occupation Sequence at Avery Island.</u> Dissertation. Louisiana State University.

Geiger, Carey L. 1980. "Survey of Selected Sites in the Leaf River Floodplain, Perry County, Mississippi." *Mississippi Archaeology, Vol. 15, No. 2.* p8-25.

Gibson, Jon L. 1975. "Fire Pits at Mount Bayou (16CT35), Catahoula Parish, Louisiana." *Louisiana Archaeology, No. 2.* p201-218.

Gibson, Jon L. 1979. "Poverty Point Trade in South Central Louisiana: An Illustration from Beau Rivage." *Louisiana Archaeology, No. 4.* p91-116.

Green, Jr., James Allen. 2020. Personal Communication, June 10, 2020.

Griffing, David L. 1985. "Surface Surveys of the Insley Site, Franklin Parish, Louisiana." *Louisiana Archaeology, No. 12.* p219-240.

Gregory, Jr., Hiram F., Lester C. Davis, Jr., and Donald G. Hunter. 1970. "The Terral Lewis Site: A Poverty Point Activity Facies in Madison Parish, Louisiana." *Southeastern Archaeological Conference Bulletin, No. 12.* p35-46. Morgantown, West Virginia.

Guderjan, Thomas H. and James R. Morehead. 1981. "Big Brushy: A Stratified Multiple Component Site at Fort Polk, Louisiana." *Louisiana Archaeology, No. 7.* p1-30.

Howard, Edgar B. 1935. <u>Evidence of Early Man in North America, Based on Geological and Archaeological Work in New Mexico.</u> Dissertation.

Hunter, Donald G. 1970. "The Catahoula Phase of the Poverty Point Complex in East-Central Louisiana." *Southeastern Archaeological Conference Bulletin, No. 12.* p73-89. Morgantown, West Virginia.

Hunter, Donald G. and William S. Baker, Jr. 1979. "Excavations in the Atkins Midden at the Troyville Site, Catahoula Parish, Louisiana." *Louisiana Archaeology, No. 4.* p21-52.

Jelks, Edward B. 1962. The Kyle Site: A Stratified Central Texas Aspect Site in Hill County, Texas. *Archaeology Series, No. 5.* Department of Anthropology, University of Texas. Austin, Texas.

Jelks, Edward B. 2017. "The Archaeology of the Sam Rayburn Reservoir." *CRHR Research Reports, Vol. 3, No. 1.*

Justice, Noel D and Suzanne K. Kudlaty. 1999. Field Guide to Projectile Points of the Midwest. Indian University Press. Bloomington, Indiana.

Kelley, J. Charles. 1947. "The Lehmann Rock Shelter: A Stratified Site on the Toyah, Uvalde, and Round Rock Foci." *Bulletin of the Texas Archaeological Society Vol. 18.* p115-128.

Kneberg, Madeline. 1956. "Some Important Projectile Point Types Found in the Tennessee Area." *Tennessee Archaeologist, Vol. 12, No. 1.* p17-27.

Krieger, Alex D. 1946. "Cultural Complexes and Chronology in Northern Texas." *University of Texas Publication No. 4640.* University of Texas. Austin, Texas.

Krieger, Alex D. 1947a. "Artifacts from the Plainview Bison Bed." In Fossil Bison and Associated Artifacts from Plainview, Texas. *Bulletin of the Geological Society of American, Vol. 58, No. 10.* p938-951.

Krieger, Alex D. 1947b. "Certain Projectile Points of the Early American Hunters." *Bulletin of the Texas Archeological Society Vol. 18.* Lubbock, Texas. p7-27.

Kuttruff, Carl. 1975. "The Poverty Point Site: North Sector Test Excavations." *Louisiana Archaeology, No. 2.* p129-151.

Lauro, James. 2008. Reconnaissance Level Cultural Resource Survey of 1,440 Acre Tract of Land for Proposed Industrial Development, Richland Parish, Louisiana. Archaeology Mississippi, Inc.

Louisiana Division of Archaeology. Louisiana Site File Database. Search query June 2020.

MacNeish, Richard S., Antoinette Nelken-Terner, and Irmgard W. Johnson. 1967. The Prehistory of the Tehuacan Valley, Volume Two: Nonceramic Artifacts. Douglas S. Byers (Ed). University of Texas Press. Austin, Texas.

Miller, E.O, and Edward B. Jelks. 1952. "Archaeological Excavations at the Belton Reservoir, Coryell County, Texas." *Bulletin of the Texas Archeological Society Vol. 23.* Lubbock, Texas. p168-217.

Neuman, Robert W. 1984. An Introduction to Louisiana Archaeology. Louisiana State University Press. Baton Rouge, Louisiana.

Newell, H. Perry, Alex D. Krieger and Volney H. Jones. 1949. The George C. Davis Site: Cherokee County, Texas. *Memoirs of the Society for American Archaeology, No. 5.* Cambridge University Press.

Perino, Gregory. 1968. Guide to the Identification of Certain American Indian Projectile Points. *Special Bulletin No. 3.* Oklahoma Anthropological Society.

Perino, Gregory. 1971. Guide to the Identification of Certain American Indian Projectile Points. *Special Bulletin No. 4.* Oklahoma Anthropological Society.

Penvy, Charlotte Donald. 2014. Exhibit U, Holly Ridge Northwest Site Historic Preservation Phase 1a. R. Christopher Goodwin & Associates, Inc.

Quimby, George I. 1957. "The Bayou Goula Site: Iberville Parish, Louisiana." *Fieldiana. Anthropology, Vol. 47, No. 2.* p91-170.

Ritchie, William A. 1971. "New York Projectile Points: A Typology and Nomenclature." *Bulletin 384.* New York State Museum.

Rolingson, Martha A. 1971. "The Ashley Point." *The Arkansas Archaeologist, Vol. 12, No. 3.* p50-52. Fayetteville, Arkansas.

Shenkel, Richard J. 1974. "Big Oak and Little Oak Islands: Excavations and Interpretations." *Louisiana Archaeology, No. 1.* p37-65.

Shenkel, Richard J. and George Holley. 1974. "A Tchefuncte House." *Southeastern Archaeological Conference Bulletin, No. 18.* p226-42. Memphis, Tennessee.

Smith, Brent W. 1975. "Patterns of the Young's Bayou Drainage, Natchitoches Parish, Louisiana." *Louisiana Archaeology, No. 2.* p163-200.

Sollberger, J.D. 1967. "A New Type Arrow Point with Speculations as to Its Origin." *The Record, Vol 23, No. 3.* Dallas Archaeological Society. Dallas, Texas.

Stephenson, Robert L. 1949. "Archaeological Survey of Lavon and Garza-Little Elm Reservoirs: A Preliminary Report." *Bulletin of the Texas Archaeological Society Vol. 20.* Lubbock, Texas. p21-62.

Suhm, Dee Ann and Alex D. Krieger. 1954. <u>An Introductory Handbook of Texas Archeology.</u> *Bulletin of the Texas Archeological Society Vol. 25.* Austin, Texas.

Taylor, Jr. Herbert C. 1948. "An Archaeological Reconnaissance in Northern Coahuila." *Bulletin of the Texas Archeological Society Vol. 19.* Lubbock, Texas. p74-87.

Ward, Trawick H., and R.P. Stephen Davis Jr. 1999. <u>Time Before History: The Archaeology of North Carolina.</u> University of North Carolina Press. Chapel Hill.

Webb, Clarence H. 1946. "Two Unusual Types of Chipped Stone Artifact." *Bulletin of the Texas Archeological Society Vol. 17.* Lubbock, Texas. p9-17.

Webb, Clarence H. 1948a. "Evidences of Pre-Pottery Cultures in Louisiana." *American Antiquity, Vol. 13, No. 3.* Lubbock, Texas. p227-232.

Webb, Clarence H. 1948b. "Caddoan Prehistory: The Bossier Focus." *Bulletin of the Texas Archaeological Society Vol. 19.* Lubbock, Texas. p100-147.

Webb, Clarence H. 1963. "The Smithport Landing Site: An Alto Focus Component in De Soto Parish, Louisiana." *Bulletin of the Texas Archaeological Society Vol. 34.* Lubbock, Texas. p143-188.

Webb, Clarence H. 1981. "Stone Points and Tools of Northwestern Louisiana." *Special Publication of the Louisiana Archaeological Society, No. 1.*

Webb, Clarence H. and Ralph R. McKinney. 1975. "Mounds Plantation (16CD12), Caddo Parish, Louisiana." *Louisiana Archaeology, No. 2.* p39-128.

Williams, Stephens and Jeffrey P. Brain. 1983. <u>Excavations at the Lake George Site: Yazoo County, Mississippi, 1958-1960.</u> *Peabody Museum Papers, Vol. 74.*

Wood, W. Raymond. 1963. "Two New Projectile Points: Homan and Agee Points." *The Arkansas Archaeologist, Vol. 4, No. 2.* p1-6. Fayetteville, Arkansas.

Woods, Michael S. 2015. "The Neches River Dart Point: Description and Clarification of a 'Relatively' New Dart Point Type." *The Journal (Houston Archeological Society), No. 135.* p11-16. Houston, Texas.

Wormington, H.M. 1957. <u>Ancient Man in North America.</u> *Denver Museum of Natural History Popular Series No. 4.* Denver Museum of Natural History. Denver, Colorado.

Wright, Newell O., Jr. 1980. "Lithics." In <u>The Hanna Site: An Alto Village in Red River Parish.</u> *Louisiana Archaeology, No. 5.* p197-225.

www.ingramcontent.com/pod-product-compliance
Lightning Source LLC
Chambersburg PA
CBHW041959150426
43194CB00002B/59